Iyanla Vanzant is the host of the daytime TV talk show *Iyanla!* and the award-winning and bestselling author of *Until Today!*, *Yesterday I Cried*, *In the Meantime*, *Every Day I Pray* and many other books. As an empowerment specialist, Spiritual Life Councillor and ordained minister, she lectures and facilitates workshops with a mission to assist in the empowerment of women and men everywhere.

OTHER BOOKS BY IYANLA VANZANT

One Day

My Soul Just

Opened Up

40 Days and 40 Nights
Toward Spiritual Strength
and Personal Growth

Iyanla Vanzant

POCKET
BOOKS

LONDON • SYDNEY • NEW YORK • TOKYO • SINGAPORE • TORONTO

First published in Great Britain by Fireside, 1998
This edition published by Pocket Books, 2002
An imprint of Simon & Schuster UK Ltd
A Viacom Company

1 3 5 7 9 10 8 6 4 2

Simon & Schuster UK Ltd
Africa House
64–78 Kingsway
London WC2B 6AH

www.simonsays.co.uk

Simon & Schuster Australia
Sydney

A CIP catalogue record for this book
is available from the British Library

ISBN 0-7434-5073-6

Printed and bound in Great Britain by
Bookmarque Ltd, Croydon

This book is dedicated to Ego,

that part of us that continues to worry,

lives in doubt,

is afraid,

judges other people,

is afraid to trust,

needs proof,

believes only when it is convenient,

fails to follow up,

refuses to practice what it preaches,

needs to be rescued,

wants to be a victim,

beats up on "self,"

needs to be right all of the time, and

continues to hold on to what does not work.

You are now put on notice that . . .

YOUR DAYS ARE NUMBERED!

Acknowledgments

In laboring with and birthing this project, I would like to acknowledge the following loving spirits:

Thank you, God! I am so grateful.

My children: Gemmia Vanzant, who gave me the title. Damon Vanzant, who is free at last! Nisa Vanzant, who is in the process of opening her soul and answering the call.

My grandchildren: Aso 'le, Oluwalomoju Adeyemi, Adesola, and Niamoja Adilah Afi, for keeping my soul open with their love.

The powerful team of women who are a constant source of strength and support: Linda Stephens, Joia Jefferson, Theresa Caldwell, Fern Robinson, Muhsinah Berry-Dawan, Cassandra Barber, Almasi Zulu, Tulani Kinard, Felicia Baldwin, Adara Walton, Helen Jones, Janet Barber, Judith Hakimah, Ebun Adelona, Coleen Goldberg, Yawfah Shakor, Lucille Gambrell, Rene Kizer, and Rev. Vivianna Hentley-Brown.

The loving men in my life who make my life as a woman a truly enjoyable and spiritual experience: Alex Morgan, Rev. Michael Beckwith, Rev. Cochise Brown, Rev. Jeremiah Wright, Rev. Frank M. Reid, III, Dr. Na'im Akbar, Dr. David Phillips, Ken Kizer, Ralph Stevenson, Basil Farrington, Ralph Blum, and Bobby Stephens.

My sister-friends who encourage me to keep at it: Susan L. Taylor, Jewel Diamond-Taylor, Tina Ansa McElroy, Bebe Moore Campbell, Maria Dowd Carothers, Jeanne Blum, and Blanche Richardson.

My spiritual mother and constant guardian, Dr. Barbara King.

My agent and ER buddy, Denise Stinson.

My editor, Dawn Daniels, who honors my process and never doubts that I will eventually do it and turn it in.

The publishing management team at Simon & Schuster who are stepping out on faith with me.

And my life partner and best friend, Adeyemi Bandele.

Thank you all for making another journey worthwhile.

First . . . words

One day my soul just opened up
   and things started happenin'
   things I can't quite explain
   I mean
   I cried and cried like never before
   I cried tears of ten thousand mothers
   I couldn't even feel anything because
   I cried 'til I was numb.

One day my soul just opened up
   I felt this overwhelming pride
   what I was proud of
   only God knows!
   Like the pride of a hundred thousand fathers
   basking in the glory of their newborn sons
   I was grinnin' from ear to ear!

One day my soul just opened up
   I started laughing
   and I laughed for what seemed like forever
   wasn't nothin' particularly funny goin' on
   but I laughed anyhow
   I laughed the joy of a million children playin'
   in the mud
   I laughed 'til my sides ached
   Oh God! It felt so good!

One day, my soul just opened up
> There were revelations, annihilations, and resolutions
> feelings of doubt and betrayal, vengeance and forgive-
> ness
> memories of things I'd seen and done before
> of places I'd been, although I didn't know when
> there were lives I'd lived
> people I'd loved
> battles I'd fought
> victories I'd won
> and wars I'd lost.

One day, my soul just opened up
> and out poured all the things
> I'd been hiding
> and denying
> and living through
> that had just happened moments before.

One day, my soul just opened up
> and I decided
> I was good and ready!
> I was good and ready
> to surrender
> my life
> to God.

So, with my soul wide open,
> I sat down
> wrote Her a note
> and told her so.

Gemmia L. Vanzant

Introduction

Removing the Veil

At one point in my life, I really thought I had it all figured out. I was working in my dream career field. I had a decent home. I was in a solid relationship. My children were being normal teenagers. Then, one morning I woke up miserable. Nothing in particular had happened. Well, actually it had. Sometime during the night, when I was asleep, I decided to tell myself the truth. I hated my job. I was lonely living in a new city where I knew no one. I was dating a married man. And I felt like I had been a horrible mother, totally incapable of ever making up to my children for the years of insanity I had inflicted upon them. People looking from the outside in thought that I had really made it! Who was I to doubt them? I convinced myself through my daily motions that they were right.

The feelings of misery, confusion, and despair began to grow like an annoying fungus in my mind. My thinking was fuzzy. I was snapping at people. I had become professionally aggressive and competitive to the point of being combative. Each day, I would push myself to exhaustion so that no more truth could be, would be, revealed to me when I was sleeping. I clung to the relationship believing that if it ended, I would surely lose my mind. It did. And I did. I lost the mind that had kept me in denial for the better part of my life. I lost the mind that was so full of distortions, half-truths, and the ideas of others that it fed my misery like a ravenous dog. I lost the mind that was angry at my mother, hated my father, resented my brother, wanted to control everything and everybody in its midst that could in any way hurt me. At the time, I didn't realize what was going on. I thought I was having a string of bad luck. As I watched my life fall to pieces, I did what any mindless person would do. I got totally pissed off! It is called *temporary insanity*.

There is something strange that happens when you go insane . . . people help you stay there! There are those who recognize your anger and support you in it. You have told them your story. They know why you are mad. What do they do? They get mad right along with you. They help you rant and rave. They even go so far as to offer you a drink in the process. Then there are those who recognize your confusion. You've told them your story too. As a matter of fact, you have probably called them every day with twisting, turning updates that keep you in a state of rage and confusion. What do they do? They offer you suggestions. They tell you what to do and what to say. At the time, it all sounds good. However, when the time comes for you to do or say what they have told you, confusion reigns supreme, insanity surfaces, and you retreat into being PO'd.

Although I did not realize it at the time, I was lucky. There was one person in my life who immediately recognized my confusion, anger, and insanity. This very astute individual went so far as to detect an even greater vulnerability. Fear. The fear that I was losing control. Fear that other people would judge me. The fear that, for some reason I was not willing to explore or mention, I was being punished. More important, this person recognized that beneath it all there was a need for me to grow. A need for me to change. They knew that I had entered a sort of spiritual twilight zone where nothing made sense, but everything was making perfect sense. I was on a journey to a place that would require boldness of heart, strength of mind, and power of spirit. This person listened to the story, offering only one seemingly useless suggestion: "Remain open. There is something bigger than you know going on here." Well, la-de-da! What the heck was that supposed to mean??

I made it through that experience. Things got better, and then they fell apart again. I changed careers. I changed partners. I cut my hair and lost thirty-two pounds. Things got better, and then they fell apart again. In the process something wonderful happened. I picked up certain abilities, habits, and practices that led me to the realization that things never really fall apart, they simply change. Somehow, even when I felt as if I was about to lose my mind (again), I could hold on to the notion that everything is always as it should be. If I was to be insane, I would just be insane. Perhaps I was sleeping when I came into the one realization that continues to sustain me: "If you know who walks beside you, you can never be afraid!" I wish I knew the exact moment and time it happened because I would have had a party. I now believe it was in that instant that my soul opened up and the spirit of the Divine entered my life.

I have met hundreds of thousands of people I recognize from my own experiences to be utterly insane. It is not the kind of insanity that will get you tossed into the looney bin. It is a kind of insanity that keeps you in a struggle for control of your life and everyone in it. The kind of insanity we are talking about here is a kind that keeps you pushing yourself, striving to do more, be better, and get ahead. Unfortunately, because you are insane, when you get ahead, when you are better, and when you get more, it is still not enough. The insanity that plagues more than half of the adult population of most countries is a kind that makes fully capable, able-bodied people stay on jobs in which they are miserable. These insane people stay in relationships where they cheat or are cheated on. They remain in situations of all kinds where they are abused, neglected, demeaned, overlooked, and, in many ways I cannot enumerate, otherwise dehumanized. The insanity I am identifying here is the kind that makes you forget *who* walks beside you and *who* lives within you and that, as a result of this loss of memory, shuts down your soul.

If you or anyone you know show signs of these symptoms, beware! This person could be walking around convinced that he or she is fine. Most insane people do that, you know. Be aware that beneath the "everything is fine" exterior, there may be a malignant fungus of fear, confusion, and misery eating away at the soul. As the soul is eaten away, each day becomes a task of drudgery. The people in the environment become crutches and victims, or perceived oppressors. If you or anyone you know is in the midst of something or everything falling apart, take heed! This could be the first sign of an insanity waiting for the opportunity to take over, cloud the mind, and destroy the spirit. If that happens, some part of you or someone you know is about to shut down. It must shut down in order for you to survive. If, on the other hand, you recognize these symptoms in yourself or someone you know, here is a piece of advice: "Remain open. There is something bigger than you know going on here."

In writing this book, it is my hope to offer support and guidance to those who are temporarily insane. I've been there, and I know it really is only temporary. Life may sometimes seem to burden us with more than we can or want to bear. It's not that we cannot handle it. It is usually that we *do not know how* to handle it. Those who are wise enough or courageous enough to pick up this book before insanity sets in will be equipped to meet the tasks that lie ahead. Those who never want to be insane again may also benefit from this therapeutic approach. No matter which category you fall in, I want to share with you the things I found to be most effective in helping me to remain open and grounded in the knowledge of who I really am when life experiences threaten to make me forget.

Forty days and forty nights spent honoring the things that really matter in life is only the first step toward personal growth and spiritual strength. If you are anything like me when I was insane, it could take you six months to complete the forty-day process. That's okay! You will do as much as you need to do, when you need it. If too much light, too much truth comes in at once, you can become spiritually blind. The good news is that when you need this book, you will have it. Gaining a working knowledge of forty spiritual principles will give you a totally new perception of yourself and life. Don't be like me when I was insane. Don't try to figure it out! New thoughts, new feelings may not show up instantly. The moment you realize that the old ways of thinking and feeling do not work for you, the process of this book will be something new for you to try. Forty days and nights may not seem like a lot; that is probably because most insane people think the more complicated a thing is, the better a thing is. That is simply not true. Forty is a mystical number. It has the power to cure insanity.

If you are willing to admit that you are or have been insane as described here and would like some help, I welcome you. If you are willing to say that it has never happened to you, but that you know people you would like to help by gaining a grasp of the information presented here, I welcome you. If you have received this book as a gift and cannot figure out why, take a hint! You are welcome here. We are about to embark upon a journey to a place where insanity will reign no more. It is a place where everything you thought you needed and wanted will fade away. It is in this place that you will find things you did not know that you had or needed. We, my dear friends, are about to enter your soul.

For some, the journey will be a quick and enjoyable one. Revelations will come. Understanding will flow. On the forty-first day you will have something to share with friends, family, and loved ones. For others, this journey will be frightening and rocky, and at times you will be convinced it is unnecessary for you to continue. You will be tempted to abort the journey. You will forget to do one assignment or another. You will convince yourself that you are not getting anything out of it. Someone may even steal your book the day before payday when you believe you cannot afford to buy another one. On that very day, something wonderful will happen to you. You will be convinced that life has really turned in your favor. On that same day, your joy will be ripped from beneath your feet and you will have forgotten to replace this book. Here again is that motto of support and encouragement for you: **"Remain open. There is something bigger than you know going on here."**

The Daily Process

Your forty-day journey will require a commitment of thirty minutes each day: twenty minutes for the morning exercise, and ten minutes for the evening exercise. Of course, you are free to spend more time than this; however, to spend less time is not advised. If your mornings are anything like mine, I would suggest doing the morning exercise as soon as you wake up, before you get "busy" doing everything else. Once you leave the bedroom, you are operating on a totally different vibration. An external vibration. Once you begin to move in the external vibration, chances are you will find every excuse in the world not to stop and pick up this book. Now that you know what could happen, you are prepared to begin. You will need this book, a pen or pencil, and two colored highlighters or colored pencils. Help yourself to stay focused and committed by placings these items at the side of your bed before retiring.

Upon waking in the morning, take five to seven deep, cleansing breaths, inhaling through the nose and exhaling through the mouth, making the sound *Ahhhhh!* Lying still on your back, focus your eyes on one spot on the ceiling. Allow your body to settle down and your breath to regain its normal pattern. When you feel ready, slowly rise to a sitting position. Work the muscles of your neck by rotating your head three or four times to the right and then the left. Take one more deep breath. You are now ready to begin.

Each of the forty principles covered is presented with a *Working Definition*. This definition is based on the universal, spiritual, or metaphysical meaning of the word. It is offered so that everyone and anyone using this process will have a common understanding of the perspective being offered. These definitions are in no way offered as an attempt to rewrite the

they presented to challenge your intellect. This book
l process, and the principles being explored and applied
m that perspective.

e working definition of the principle, continue reading
on the principle of the day. Use one colored highlighter or
pencil to   e anything you read that rings familiar or true to you, and
anything presented that is totally new to you. Use another colored highlighter or pencil to identify anything you read to which you feel resistance,
those things that sound totally farfetched and crazy. After reading the
Commentary, turn to the page entitled *Commentary Journal*. This page is
offered so that you can document your immediate response and reaction to
what you have read. It may also be helpful to write down those things you
have highlighted and the impressions or feelings they arouse in you.
Following each Commentary Journal, you will find a *Morning Affirmation*.
This is an affirmative prayer offered to assist you in integrating the principle into your consciousness. The Morning Affirmation is a powerful tool
that will alert your mind as to what you intend to experience throughout
the day. Feel free to read it, silently or aloud, as many times as you like.
You may also want to highlight those things that make the greatest impression on you. Once you have read the Morning Affirmation, spend a few
moments in silence, allowing what you have read to become integrated into
your mind. This is a perfect time to say a silent prayer for yourself or someone else. The reading exercise combined with the prayer are excellent ways
to direct your will and focus your energy. You are now ready to begin your
day. Once you get the hang of it, this entire process should take no more
than twenty minutes.

Whether you choose to carry this book with you or leave it at home, an
entry has been included that will help you integrate the day's principle into
your activities. The pages entitled *Let Me Remember* . . . contain a series of
statements of the ideas contained in the day's Commentary that will help
you remember the day's principle. If you carry the book with you, you can
read them as often as you need them. If you do not carry the book, it may
be helpful to write these statements down on an index card and stick them
in your purse or pocket. They are like a "booster shot" that will help you
practice the principle for the day.

The evening process is relatively simple. Before retiring for the evening,
reread the Commentary. Mentally reviewing your day, remind yourself of
the ways in which you were able to apply the principle, and the ways in

which you were not. Identify any evidence you discovered that the principle worked, and the ways in which the principle seemed not to work. You are now ready to complete the *Evening Journal*. Once again, the questions and statements in the Evening Journal are offered as a guide, concepts to help you focus. Feel free to write whatever comes up for you regarding the principle, how it did or did not apply to your experiences of the day, or what you are feeling at the moment. It is all relative to your journey. Through this writing process, the principle takes shape and form, and becomes a tangible element you can work with or work through.

Once you complete the Evening Journal, you are finished with the principle. If you feel incomplete or that you need to continue working with a particular principle, go for it! Begin the process with the same principle when you awake the next day. If you feel complete, you are free to begin working with the next commentary.

Of course, you can ignore this suggested process and choose whatever principle you feel best suits your needs on any particular day. You can also work with any one or two principles for as long as you feel necessary. Don't be alarmed if you did not seem to get it, or if you cannot stay peaceful, non-resistant, and fearless about exploring a particular principle and applying it to your life experiences. Your mind is being opened to a new perspective that will facilitate growth whether or not you are aware of it, feel it, or believe it. The truth of the matter is, none of this is new. You already know everything being presented to you. You are actually being guided in remembering what was etched into your soul long ago.

There is one precaution I will offer. You can expect your life to change a great deal as you begin to integrate these principles. Unfortunately, the change may not always look or feel very nice. That too is part of the process. Learning, understanding, or practicing spiritual disciplines will not immunize you against any of the lessons you must "grow through" in your life. Doing a new thing, thinking a new way, actively applying this information to your life and experiences is a profound learning process. As you persist through the process, learning to integrate the information, one principle will become reliant on another until they all mesh together into a cohesive workable foundation of thought. You will remember what your spiritual foundation is and was always meant to be. Your foundation. This foundation will give you the strength to work through new experiences, and the courage to face the "outworking" of old ones.

When your life and this process are working, it may feel as if nothing is going on. That's good! When your life is working there will be an absence of drama. In the absence of drama, conflict, and chaos, lasting change is given the opportunity to take place. As always, I encourage you to be patient with yourself. Be gentle with yourself. Know that all things are working in your favor. If you take one step toward the light of Spirit, Spirit will take five steps on your behalf.

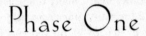

Phase One

Dear God,
Speak into my words today.
Think into my thoughts today.
Work in all my deeds today.
I am Yours to use, today and forever.
And So It Is!

Honor the Divine

I can imagine that I am not alone when I say I have spent the majority of my life being angry with God. The time that I did not spend being angry I spent being totally confused, and when I wasn't confused I was afraid. Growing up in the church as I did, I came to know God as an amorphous, external entity. He was big, He was fierce, He was waiting for me to mess up so He could swoop down and get me. Getting me had to do with making me suffer and taking away things that I loved and wanted, like my mother. Getting me had to do with never approving of me or accepting me because of all the bad, inappropriate, or purely human things that I was prone to do. Somewhere in my life, I grew to understand that God was not happy with me. That was just fine, because I wasn't too thrilled about Him either!

What does it mean to believe in God? My childhood perception of God, that He was everywhere and could see everything, followed me well into adulthood. *He* saw me steal the candy. *He* saw me kiss those boys. *He* knew that I used four-letter words, smoked, drank, and had been promiscuous. *He* knew that I had lied to my boss (killing off my grandmother and any other spare relatives), my children, and the IRS, and, of course, *He* knew that I had lied to my mother many, many times. *He* was really mad at me and for that reason, and for many other reasons, I was afraid of Him. His anger, I concluded, was evidenced by the ongoing drama and crisis in my life—*He* let me get pregnant at sixteen. *He* allowed me to marry a man who beat me, left me, came back to beat me, then cheat on me, only to again leave me. *He* let me be hungry and homeless. *He* refused to hire me for that job I really needed. Yes, God and I were rarely on speaking terms, and when we were, *He* always seemed to be punishing me for something I had done or not done. I couldn't figure out which it was. Whatever His reasons, He was really testing my beliefs.

I kept trying to get on God's good side. I knew all the perfunctory prayers. The Twenty-third Psalm. The Lord's Prayer. With a little help, I could even follow the Ninety-first Psalm without reading it from the Bible. Actually, I would say the words I knew out loud and allow my mouth to move while mumbling all the others. I knew the songs, those spirituals that seemed to have so much meaning, to give such great comfort to so many. "Precious Lord Take My Hand." "Amazing Grace." "Nearer My God to Thee." "What a Friend We Have in Jesus." Jesus! Oh Lord, let's not go there! Just the mere mention of Him caused me to become paralyzed by fear. But I would sing even those songs, the Jesus-filled songs, real loud when I was trying to impress God. I thought I could make God believe that I really knew and trusted Him. I also knew how to console other people who seemed to be in conflict with or about God. I would tell them that God knew best. I knew how to impress those people, telling them I would pray for them. I thought I really knew how to pray. I had heard my grandmother and the other "saints" in the church do it, and I followed their lead. I knew how to do all the things I had been taught would make God happy with me, but somewhere, deep inside, I knew I was just playing a game. I really wanted to believe in God, but I couldn't figure out what that meant.

Grandma always said, "Never take the Lord's name in vain!" and "Don't tempt the Lord!" This, among many other seemingly meaningless religious practices, is what led to a great deal of my confusion. If God was everywhere and had so much power, didn't He know I was already mad, confused, afraid? And if He did, why didn't he "strike me dead!" like Grandma believed was about to happen at any moment? If God were so lovingly concerned about me, why didn't He help me, stop me, give me better guidance? Why did God allow bad things to happen to good people? And when bad people tried to be good, why did they have to be punished? I *wanted* an answer to these questions; however, I *needed* an answer to the lifelong inquisition, what does it mean to believe in God? It was a bit much to try to figure out. So I, like many others, I suspect, shut down, tuned out, turned off to God. Boy, did that feel better! Just do what you have to do when you have to do it, without being afraid of what might happen. I thought it was a relief. It seemed to make sense to me, and it reinforced the underlying belief that God was only available to certain people. Certain special people of whom I was not one.

I wish I could pinpoint the day it all turned around for me. I wish I could identify the book that I read. The song that I heard. The words that rang loud and true in my mind that answered all the questions and gave me a totally different outlook on the presence of God in my life as something Divine. I can imagine that it was a time when I was in trouble. I will admit that no matter what I thought I believed, when I was in deep do-do, I went back, crawling on my belly like a reptile, to God. I think I am the author of the prayer, "God, if you help me this time, I promise never to bother you again! And this time I really mean it!" I have never been really ill, which means it was not the fear of death or the need for a physical healing. My children have never been in peril either, so that could not have been the impetus prompting the rekindling of my relationship. I know it was not the quest for money. I lived in poverty most of my life and had decided long ago that God does not give money to poor people. I don't think it was begging for the return of a lover. Or the great escape from some predicament of emotional despair. As best as I can recall, the day I actually felt the presence of the Divine in my life, it was a quiet knowing in my heart. Or maybe it was a profound thought that guided me to do something that changed my life forever. Whatever it was, whenever it happened, it was an experience that let me know without a shadow of a doubt that me and *He* were finally all right. I also know that it was that experience which taught me that to believe in God is to recognize and acknowledge God's divine presence within yourself.

Today, after many years of self-torment acknowledging all the foolish choices and bad decisions I once made, I now know that "God is in the midst of me and God believes in me." Thank you, Charles Filmore, founder of Unity Village. I now believe with all my heart that "there is but one Mind and we are each a manifestation of that Mind, the mind of God, the Divine." I also believe that we are each a unique expression of the Divine Mind living to fulfill a divine mission and purpose. As an expression of that one Divine Mind, there is nothing we need or need to know that is beyond our immediate recognition. Thank you Ralph Emerson, Joel Goldsmith,

Howard Thurman, Eric Butterworth, Emilie Cady, and Elvis Presley for the work you have done and the words you have spoken that brought this to my attention. Today, even when I am experiencing despair, confusion, or a seeming calamity in my life, I know, "The Father knows my needs even before I ask!" Thank you, Jesus! I finally realize you are not out to get me, you are walking with me, and that our Father loves me as much as He loved you. Most of all, I thank the Spirit within me for teaching me, showing me, being patient with me as I lived through the self-imposed punishment that eventually opened my heart and mind to the presence of the Spirit, the one Mind that is greater than I.

What does it mean to believe in God? It means learning to honor your own inherent Godliness. This is not an easy task, but it is worth every ounce of effort you expend. Even though I now know what it means to believe and accept the presence of the Divine as an inherent part of my being, there are times when I slip back into my old fears, old beliefs, and old confusion. I admit there are moments when I focus on the problem and not on the presence of goodness that is God. Today, however, I know how to get still, ask the question, and listen for the answer, because I always try to remember, "Right where I am, God is, and God believes in me." It is in these moments when the intellectual mind becomes still that the Spirit will unfold and soar. It is when you can make these quiet pronouncements with belief that the presence of the Divine is activated, infusing your being with a sense of peaceful well-being. I have learned that there is no magic formula that will bring you to that moment. Nor is there one particular way to get there. There is, however, one requirement that seems to be true for everyone. You must have a deep desire to know the Divine that is not based on anything other than the deep desire. You cannot want it for any other reason other than to want it. It is just that simple.

What does it mean to believe in God and embrace that divine presence? It means you will still stumble at times, forgetting what you want, falling headfirst into the old habits and beliefs. Fear not! That is to be expected. Whenever you challenge the old ways with new ways, the old ways will fight you tooth and nail. Always remember to be patient and loving with yourself and others because that is what God does all the time. There will be moments when fear will overtake you, cut your breath off, and make your head spin. The fear of losing control, of being weird, of giving up the familiar and comfortable for what is surely to be unfamiliar and uncomfortable. A mentor once told me, "When you are comfortable, you are not growing!" If you want to grow into a divine space in life, you must breathe (*Ahhhhh!*) and keep moving forward.

Rest assured there will be times when you fall flat on your face. It will seem as if the harder you pray, the more you attempt to trust, the more holy and devout you become, the worse your life will appear to be. Things that were going well will go wrong. Things that were not going so well will blow up in your face. It is a trick! Do not be fooled by appearances! Hold on to the words, the phrase, the prayer, the little bits of trust and faith you can muster. You are not being tested! You are being fortified! Remember, you cannot fail! All paths lead to the same road. The road to peace, joy, and the memory of God's unconditional love.

Why, you ask, would you want to take the journey? Why would you look for God when you are doing just fine? You are making it on what you know, what you have learned. Why would God help you now? And what's in it for you? I have asked those questions of myself many, many times. I have found many answers. Some of the answers emerged from the old school, the old belief system that kept me in fear and confusion. If I didn't go to God, He would someday come to "get me"! There were many times I tried desperately to convince myself to believe. God is good! God knows best! Even with this in my arsenal, when things did not go the way I thought they should go, I became angry and frightened. The one answer to all of my questions that has stuck with me the longest and made the greatest impression has been, "God is as dependent on you as you are on God!" The Creator of the universe, the divine energy of life, needs me to demonstrate the goodness S/He has in store for all people. "I am the light of the world," and God wants me to shine in the glory of this knowledge. God believes I can do it. When it was put to me that way, I figured I had very little to lose and everything in the world to gain. With a little faith, trust, and effort, I know you will discover that the same is true for you.

DAY 1

Honor the Divine
with . . . TRUTH

Working Definition:

The principle we are working with today is TRUTH. It is the Absolute, that which reveals and is in accord with the will of the Divine as the governing principle of life. Truth is eternal, the same today as yesterday. The fullness of truth related to the Divine exists at the core of every living being. The basic principle of truth is that the mind of every individual is unified with Divine Mind eternally. As individual awareness expands and embraces the concept of divine truth, understanding unfolds.

Commentary on Truth

I had so many lies in my foundation. My mother, bless her heart, told me what she thought I needed to know to make it in life. These things that she told me constituted my armor, my protection from the harshness of the world. Unfortunately, Mother dear, what you told me had nothing to do with the truth of my being. It was painful for me to accept this fact, that my mother was in essence a liar. It was even more difficult for me to wade through mother's instructions and find the truth, God's truth. It meant that I had to examine everything that I had been told and weigh it against the universal truth. It was most unfortunate that even that truth was skewed by the church, the evening news, and Captain Kangaroo.

It's hard out there! No one is going to give you anything! You've got to work hard for what you want in this life! Don't trust people! People will step on you if you don't watch out. You've got to be better than everyone else! If you don't stand out no one will notice you! This is what my parents and their friends pounded into my head. Underlying it all were their low expectations of me and for me because I was a woman. I'm sure my mother, father, and grandmother thought they were giving it to me straight, and I believed they were. Unfortunately, their instructions, integrated with my own perceptions, resulted in massive confusion.

I must say that even in their protective hysteria, there were a few gems my caregivers gave me that have proven to be as lasting and empowering as they were originally confusing and disempowering. In particular, "Follow your first thought." My interpretation, "Why the hell should I listen to me? I am wretched! Born of the original sin! Only certain people get God's attention, and most of them are men. I'm too young! I don't know enough! I'm a woman!" Then there is the classic, "Do unto others as you would have them do unto you." Wait just a frinkin' minute here! Are others the same people who are waiting to do me in? Pounce on me? Betray my trust? Take what I have and leave me high and dry? What am I supposed to do unto them if not protect myself from them? Lest we forget, "Jesus died for your sins. You must receive Him as your savior if you want to get to Heaven." I don't know about most people, but I was raised to fear death. The thought that I had done something, anything, particularly something I was totally unaware of, that cost someone else their life left me riddled with guilt. Now, when I'm guilty, I have a hard time facing the people who remind me of what I have done or not done to be guilty about. Besides that, those childhood images of Christ hanging on the cross reminded me of my guilt and also told me that he hadn't made out so well. How was he going to help me from the position he was in? The messages. The images. The conflict within myself led me further away from the place I wanted to be, standing in truth.

"You must do your own independent investigation of truth." Powerful words from a friend teaching me about the Baha'i faith are a good starting point for the journey to uncovering truth. When you are courageous enough to examine and challenge those things that you have been taught to accept as truth, you cannot help but find the truth beneath their accepted meaning. Discovering and embracing just one eternal truth will fill your heart, bring tears to your eyes, and eradicate the false beliefs in an instant. How will you know it when you find it? "The sheep always know the voice of the Shepherd!" More important, just like our mothers told us, "The truth will set you free!" The truth will bring you back to the place you started as a divine idea in the mind of God. The truth will free you from the habitual fears the process of life can impose upon you. The truth will eliminate your need to be anything other than what you already are . . . *Divine*. It will prove to be an adequate and fulfilling substitution for the need to scratch, claw, and fight to get anything. The truth is, we already have everything we need. The truth, in its most simple form, is an exorcist for the "spirit of the do-do"—do this, do that, do it now, do it fast. The truth allows you to just *Be*. The ability to *be* okay with who you are, doing whatever it is that you are doing, in any given moment, is the piece of heaven we spend our lives killing ourselves to find. The results of an independent investigation for truth is the only incontrovertible proof that truth is eternal, consistent, dependable, and born of love. For me, the discovery of *the truth about truth* was enough to enable me to forgive my well-intentioned mother and, for that matter, everyone else who had supported me in my misconceptions about life or myself.

Truth Postulates

My own independent investigation of truth eventually resulted in my ability to embrace certain ideas that were consistent, although hard to find. In every religious text, every book on personal growth, every "new age" treatise I examined, there were certain theories that kept popping up. Of course, they were all said in a different way. Some of them were presented as the deep, underlying meaning of some entertaining story. Other statements of truth were simply glaring at me as if daring me to challenge them. I did and they won! It seems to me that no matter how they are framed or presented, certain consistent ideas emerged about life that made it seem worth living. I call these *Truth Postulates*.

POSTULATE 1
God is Life. God is Spirit. God is Mind. God is the only power that is in control of life, spirit, and mind.

POSTULATE 2
God is within you and every living thing. Translated, this means that everything living is a unique representation of God's identity—mind, spirit, and life.

POSTULATE 3
We've got nothing but time, and it is on our side. This is why we continue to be provided with the opportunity to repeat and re-create in our lives.

POSTULATE 4
God does not punish us. We punish ourselves with guilt, shame, and fear when we choose not to act in concert with our inherently divine nature.

POSTULATE 5
There is a Divine Order to everything in life. It is for this reason that exactly where you are at any given time in life is exactly where you should be according to the Divine unfolding of your consciousness and life.

POSTULATE 6
Life is the unfolding of experiences designed to bring to our awareness the impersonal operation of the universal principles sometimes called natural laws. When we are aware that the principles are operating and govern ourselves to live in harmony with them, it becomes easy to understand the experiences we have in life.

POSTULATE 7
God doesn't bless people. We receive the grace of the Divine as abundance, peace, joy, well-being, and love as a function of what we think, feel, and believe about life, ourselves, and the Divine.

POSTULATE 8
Our lives are a reflection of our conscious and subconscious choices. When we do not choose, we live by default.

POSTULATE 9
Everybody is born to fulfill a divine purpose, and God has given us everything we will ever need to fulfill that purpose.

Everyone will discover the degree of truth that supports what they believe about life, just as I did. I guess the most difficult challenge we all face is learning to live what we believe each day, all the time, under all circumstances. People don't always act like they are representatives of God. There are times when punishment is the only logical rationale you can find for what you are experiencing. Deadlines and demands seem to restrict your time. They do not give you more of it. When you try to substitute "man's law" for Divine Law there seems to be a very inequitable distribution of goods and resources. If you were to actually do unto others what it appears that they are doing to you, there is a very good chance you would be carted off to the nuthouse, if not to jail. How could I be expected to really apply these things to my life when everyone around me is doing life the way life has always been done—as fast as possible, by any means necessary, get it done at all costs, so that it costs you little or nothing? The answer, as simple as it seems, absolutely works. "Behold! I do a new thing! I live the truth of the universe!" By holding on to the perfect, immutable truth of the Divine and incorporating it into every aspect of your being and your life, you are freed from the chains of the habit. By reminding yourself daily that you are a perfect and unique representative of all that God is, you will find that you are equipped to handle anything. This process will help you remember and practice the truth of your soul.

Commentary Journal

After reading today's commentary, I realize

The key phrase(s) I want to remember and work with today are

Morning TRUTH Affirmation

Today, I ask that the TRUTH be revealed to me.

TRUTH is eternal. TRUTH is the essence of my soul. TRUTH is my connection to the divine source of all life.

Today, I welcome the presence of TRUTH as the universal intelligence that knows exactly what I must do in every situation, under all circumstances.

No matter what appears before me today, I know there is a greater TRUTH grounded in love, power, peace, joy, and wisdom that will guide and protect me.

Today, I invoke the presence of TRUTH as the light that will cast out all thoughts of separation, limitation, and confusion.

The light of TRUTH now infuses my mind, reminding me that there is a power and a presence of the Divine that is greater than any physical problem.

Today, I speak the TRUTH. I hear the TRUTH. I see the greater, divine TRUTH of every situation I encounter.

The TRUTH that is divine, eternal, all-knowing, and ever-present now frees me to live fully, completely, and abundantly.

I am grateful for the TRUTH that is now revealed to me this day.

And So It Is!

Let Me Remember . . .

God is TRUTH. TRUTH is divine.

TRUTH is eternal and consistent. It never changes.

God is within every living thing, which means there is a divine and eternal TRUTH beneath everything I see.

TRUTH is greater than any problem on the physical level.

The TRUTH is that God believes in me.

Evening TRUTH Journal

I, _____ , *am open to know the TRUTH about myself as it* relates to

I, _____ , *am open to know the TRUTH as it relates to*

I, _____ , *accept as TRUTH that I*

DAY 2

Honor the Divine
with . . . TRUST

Working Definition:

The principle we are working with today is TRUST. It is reliance upon the Divine for all sustenance and supply. A mental and emotional recognition and acceptance that the presence of the Divine as the ultimate good is all-powerful and everywhere present.

Commentary on TRUST

There is a big difference between *trusting* somebody and *putting your trust in* somebody. At first, it was difficult for me to see the difference. However, after several painful heartbreaks and a myriad of disappointments, the difference became crystal clear. When you *trust* someone, you recognize them as a representative of divine energy. You see them in the highest light possible, knowing that no matter what they may do, it does not change who they are at the core of their being. Nor can anything that happens to you change who you are at your core. You are not reliant on people. You have learned to rely on the divine presence within them. You know with them and for them that the eternal light of truth in their soul will shine forth . . . eventually.

When you *put your trust in* someone it means that you expect them to do what they say they will do, which is usually something that you should be doing for yourself. Trusting *in* someone usually means that there is something they have that you believe you need, or something you have that you believe they can take away to cause you harm. You place your reliance on words or promised action rather than the Divine. Knowing full well that human beings are subject to do many things and anything in response to their internal fear, guilt, or shame, why do we place our trust in one another? Why? Because we forget to invoke the Divine presence in all circumstances. Even when we do invoke the Divine and our trust is betrayed, we blame the human being rather than embracing the experience as a lesson of the Divine.

My first experience of trying to explain the difference to someone was a very difficult one. A friend of mine had a brother who was addicted to drugs. She had tried on many occasions to support him through rehabilitation. Every attempt failed. After several months of being absent from the family, the brother reappeared one day. He looked healthy and clean. He assured his sister that he was "trying" to stay clean. He told her he needed a place to stay. Her own fear, guilt, and shame inspired her to welcome her brother to her couch. Over the next several weeks, he "tried" to find a job. She was doing her best to support him with food, clothing, and spending money. One bright Saturday morning, she left her brother asleep to go run errands. When she arrived home in the late afternoon, she found her television, stereo, two cameras, several exquisite pieces of jewelry, fur coat, and brother gone.

My friend was devastated. Her brother had betrayed her trust. No, I assured her, he had acted in accordance with the human condition of being chemically addicted. He had not really done anything to her. Everything that was stolen could be replaced. It was not a pleasant experience. But why had she expected anything different? She couldn't explain it. A person who is *trying* is not doing. Either you *are* or you *are not* a particular thing. There is nothing between doing and not doing that can be trusted. She couldn't hear me. She had done everything in her power, she said, to help him and protect herself. She didn't mind that he had stolen the television from the living room. It was old and beat up, not worth much even on the street. He, however, had jimmied the lock on her bedroom door, and that is where he found her "good" stuff. If she trusted her brother, I asked, why did she have a lock on her bedroom door? The truth of the matter is, she really did not trust him. She had put her trust *in* what he had said, rather than trust the divine wisdom that motivated her to lock the door. That wisdom was telling her that her brother was still capable of theft.

Trust is not something people must earn from us. Nor is it something we give to people who have proven themselves worthy. Trust is divine, a given inherent in our soul. Every living being as a manifestation of divine energy is worthy of being trusted. Either you trust or you do not trust. Trust requires reliance upon divine wisdom to demonstrate itself as the actions we take. There are many situations and people that demonstrate that it is not wise to place your trust in them. In these cases, our own innate wisdom, sometimes called intuition, will give us an internal signal. We will feel uneasy, pressured, conflicted. We will be resistant to moving forward or relying on what we hear or see. Rather than trust ourselves and the Divine within us, we will fall prey to our human senses and sympathies, cast wisdom to the wind and become victims of poor judgment.

Trust the Divine to provide for you everything you need to live fully, peacefully, and abundantly. This does not mean that people will always do the divine or right thing. But remember, you are not putting your trust in people, you are trusting that the Divine will manifest through people. It does not mean that your car will not be stolen or your purse snatched. It does mean that you can trust that you will not be harmed, and that whatever you lose will be replaced. Trust the Divine to provide you with the wisdom to make the right decision under every circumstance you encounter. If you want to know what to do, you must ask, quietly in your heart. Once you do, you will be guided. You will be protected. It may not always seem like what you are doing at the moment is the right thing. People and conditions may challenge you. You may begin to doubt yourself. It is in these moments that you are called upon to activate your trust in the Divine. Rely on what your heart tells you is true. Do not be afraid to see the truth in the situation and act accordingly. Trusting the Divine has one very important aspect that is sure to have a positive impact on your life: Learning to recognize and interpret the signs and signals you will surely receive will teach you to trust yourself.

After reading today's commentary, I realize

The key phrase(s) I want to remember and work with today are

Morning TRUST Affirmation

Today, I place my TRUST in the omnipresence of the Divine.
I TRUST that I will be divinely guided today.
I TRUST that I will be divinely protected today.
I TRUST that everything that concerns me will be brought into divine
    order according to the perfect will of the Divine.
I TRUST that my experiences today will provide me with divine revela-
    tions that lead to divine understanding and that will unfold as divine
    wisdom, as an active faculty present in my consciousness.
I TRUST that all my needs will be met today.
I TRUST that the pure desires of my heart will manifest today.
I TRUST that the loving presence of the Divine will sustain this day, as it
    has every day before this day, and as it will forever.
I am grateful that my TRUST in all that is good, God, and the Divine is
    the only sustenance I will ever need.
And So It Is!

Let Me Remember . . .

TRUST of the Divine is not the same as TRUST in people.

TRUST is an instrument of divine wisdom.

TRUST is the reliance on the Divine to provide all things.

TRUST cannot be broken. It is given in wisdom or in shame, guilt, or fear.

TRUST in Self is TRUST in the Divine.

Today, I found it difficult to TRUST when

Today, I found it easy to TRUST when

Today, I realize I find it difficult to TRUST myself when

DAY 3

Honor the Divine with ... PRAYER

Working Definition:

The principle we are working with today is communion. PRAYER is a form of communion. It is the method of communication between man and the Divine. An inward exploration undertaken to cleanse and perfect consciousness. An act of reaching in to the Higher Self.

Commentary on PRAYER

Most of us have some pretty definite ideas about prayer. We learned them from our parents. We learned them in church. We read accounts of how prayer changed people or situations. At one time, I thought prayer was something that had to be done on your knees at the side of the bed. That notion was shattered when I discovered prayer in the church, done aloud, sometimes very loud, which could eventually lead to the laying on of hands and other healing acts. In the many classes, workshops, seminars, and lectures I have attended, I learned to pray quietly, affirmatively, and as an act of intercession for others. I have also learned to pray *over* things, *in* things, *because of* things, and *in the midst* of things. More important, I was taught to pray *for* things. When all is said and done, I have discovered that prayer is a very personal and intimate act. How you pray, when you pray, and why you pray is a direct reflection of your understanding of the Divine and the role that understanding plays in your life.

Prayer is the most highly effective spiritual act one can perform. Prayer, done as an active demonstration of your belief in the presence of God, accelerates the mental and emotional energy within your being. The language of prayer, whether it is done in supplication (asking for something) or affirmation (declaring that something is already done) helps to bring the mental, physical, and emotional bodies into alignment. These bodies, commonly referred to as mind, body, and spirit, ignite the energy of the Divine when they are in alignment. While most of us believe this divine energy exists outside of us and goes about doing our bidding, the truth of the matter is, this energy is within us. Prayer, therefore, brings us into alignment with what already exists within us and opens our minds to the revelation of this existence in the outer world. In other words, what we pray for, we already have; but in most cases, we are not aware of it.

In my most insane moments, I have prayed for some pretty wild things. Money. Love. For someone else to be harmed. For a loved one to be saved from some tragedy. For someone not to die. In every situation, my prayers were answered. Unfortunately, I usually didn't recognize the answer when it showed up. After years of complaining that God does not answer my prayers, I realized that God always answers prayers! According to principles of truth, according to Divine Will for my highest good, and according to my faith (which we will explore later), I always received an answer. Now here's the catch. When I did not allow thoughts of doubt to enter my mind, my prayers were answered. When I really expected a positive outcome, my prayers were answered. When I was very specific about what I wanted, my prayers were answered. When I stopped blaming God and other people for everything that was wrong with my life and became willing to accept responsibility for my life, my prayers were answered quickly!

I was in a tight financial jam and called a dear friend asking her to pray with me that the money would show up. We prayed and hung up. Moments later she called back and said, "You know, we keep praying to a God outside of us asking Him to come and do something for us. I think that is the result of what we were taught in the Western religious philosophy. In the Eastern philosophy, we are taught that the spirit of the Divine is already within us. Our job is to acknowledge its presence, and ask that power to manifest in us and through us to give us the strength to do whatever it is we need to do. We know what to do. We simply need the strength to do it. My prayer is for you to acknowledge your own divinity, and to call it forth as your strength." She was so absolutely right, I cried.

Where are we taught that prayer is something we can go to at any time, in any place? Are we ever taught that in order to get results, we must pray a certain way, with faith and persistence? I will be among the first to admit that for many years my prayers were results-oriented. There was something I wanted, and I thought prayer could get it for me when I could not get it for myself. It took me quite some time to realize that prayer is actually *an affirmation of what already exists*. Prayer is a demonstration of our willingness to receive what exists as an outgrowth of our faith in the truth that it is good for us. Prayer is an acknowledgment of our trust in the Divine to provide everything we need, when we need it. Even a prayer of supplication or asking is an affirmative statement that we are open and ready to receive. When we pray, we are asking for the intervention of Spirit on our behalf or on behalf of someone else. Spiritual intervention is always a divine win-win situation that will unfold in a divine manner according to divine will.

When we do not understand who we truly are we generally miss the true meaning of prayer. *"Call forth the Divine within as the strength you need in order to do what you know you must do."* If you must make a decision, call forth the Divine. If you must resolve a conflict, call forth the Divine. If you need healing, financial supply, strength, or wisdom, call forth the Divine. Know that what you need already exists within you, and perhaps you simply are not aware of its existence around you. Call forth the Divine within not so that you can get something, rather so that you can realize something. Call forth the Divine, not by begging or pleading, rather with trust that when you call It will show up. Call forth the Divine not because you don't know what else to do, rather because you know what to do and need the spiritual strength to do it. Prayer is a calling forth of the Divine that results in your mind, body, and spirit being brought into alignment with exactly what you need in any given moment.

After reading today's commentary, I realize

The key phrase(s) I want to remember and work with today are

Morning PRAYER Affirmation

The divine source of all life is the fulfillment of all potential.
I believe that the divine energy of universal intelligence is guiding me now.
*I believe that the divine source of universal supply is fulfilling my every
    need now.*
*I believe that the divine presence of wholeness and well-being fills my
    being now.*
I know what the Divine knows.
I have what the Divine owns.
I am what the Divine is.
I know this to be the truth of my being.
I accept this truth as the will of the Divine.
*I trust the one Life, one Mind, one Power, one Presence to manifest at its
    fullest potential and fulfill every desired good in my heart.*
I am so grateful for the knowledge of this truth as it unfolds.
And So It Is!

Let Me Remember . . .

I have the power to call forth the Divine.

Every PRAYER is answered according to Divine Will.

Everything I need I already have.

Everything I need to know I already know.

PRAYER brings me into alignment with my good.

I trust that I will recognize the answer to my PRAYER when it shows up.

Today, I remembered to call forth the Divine when

Today, I was able to recognize Divine presence as/when

Today, it was easy/difficult for me to pray when

DAY 4

Honor the Divine
with . . . MEDITATION

Working Definition:

The principle we are working with today is STILLNESS. It is accomplished through the act of meditation, which is stilling of the physical/conscious mind to all external stimuli. Continuous, contemplative thought given to truth. A steady effort of the mind to know and hear the voice of God from within the being. The act of "not doing" in an attempt to expand the awareness of "being." When we quiet the conscious mind to hear the Divine presence.

Commentary on MEDITATION

In the beginning, we are tiny little beings with no eyes, ears, noses, or mouths. This means we are quiet. We don't know whether we are black or white, male or female, rich or poor, attractive or not. We do not work, but we do not think of ourselves as being lazy or nonproductive. We have no responsibilities to or for ourselves or others. We are not consciously aware that we know anything. Since we don't know that we know, we do not think of ourselves as being inferior for not knowing. In the beginning we are content to grow into life, into being. People understand that we are in a growth process, and they leave us alone, to grow on our own.

If we are lucky in our do-nothing, know-nothing state, the people who know about us, those who know we are growing, are happy for us and about us. They love us, sight unseen. If we are not so lucky, the people who know about us may be quite upset, frantic as a matter of fact, but it doesn't matter. We will still grow. There is a power, a force of life in and around us that loves us even though the people around us are frantic. It is that force of life around us that helps us to grow. The help is free. It asks for nothing in return. And you know what? Even though we look pretty weird floating around in the dark, the force stays with us, showering us with love. It is this force of life that ensures that all of our important parts are in the right places. It is this energy of life that makes sure we have enough to eat. This forceful energy protects us in the dark. Moves us through it while we are on the inside so that we can make it on the outside. The energy I am referring to, the energy that has been with us and in us since our beginning, is the spirit of the Divine.

Once we are born, we forget all about this divine energy of life that once put us together. Perhaps it is because we cannot see this energy with our eyes. It is much like the currents of electricity that move through the wires of the television. We plug the set in, push the "on" button, and presto!— there's the picture. We know there is a hidden power at work, but we don't really think about it. We hardly ever talk about it. We also know that if we do not plug the television set in or turn it on it will do absolutely nothing. We realize that the invisible presence of electricity will produce what it is we desire. The power of the Divine works in exactly the same manner. Its invisible presence is the energy we need in order to be activated. Just like the television, you must first be idle in order to be activated. When a television is activated it will produce currents of sound that can be heard and light that can be seen. You, on the other hand, must turn off all currents of sound and light in order to get plugged in. The act of meditation is the best way to get plugged in and turned on to the power of the Divine.

Go back to the beginning. Have no eyes, no ears, no voice. Know nothing. Do nothing. Be nothing. This is the best description of meditation I can offer. You must be able to allow yourself to float in a sea of darkness. This means you must learn to let go. Let go of all thoughts about yourself, your responsibilities in life, opinions about yourself, your desires, and the fear. Meditation enables you to let go of what you know. In order to meditate, you must accept that the invisible power, the force of life that moves through you, will provide everything you need. Think of it this way: You floated around in the darkness of the womb for nine months and turned out okay. Is it so difficult to return to that state for five, ten, or fifteen minutes a day? Is it not worth a try?

I have not kept count of the number of times people have said to me, "I don't know how to meditate." Or, "It's hard to meditate. I feel stupid just sitting there doing nothing!" For those who feel that way, I offer this suggestion. You are not "doing nothing." You are plugging in. You are activating the power. You are remembering from whence you came. You are moving yourself out of the way and allowing the divine force of life to move into your being. It will be difficult only if you think of it as difficult. When I first started to meditate, I had an elaborate plan. Candles. Incense. A special mat and a garment. It would take me twenty minutes to get ready to sit down. Once I did, I had expectations. I wanted to float like the swami I had once studied with. My goal was to focus my energy and attention to such a degree that my 140-pound butt would be lifted off the mat. Needless to say, it never happened. It did not because I was busy trying to make it happen. I took a desire into the act of meditation that kept my mind so occupied that it never got still enough for me to plug into the power that would help me float.

"Be still and know!" Stillness is the key. Still the mind. Still the body. Still the need to be anything in order to get plugged in. Once you are plugged in, the power is activated. The energy begins to move. Anything you need to know, you will know. If there is anything you need to do, you will be instructed. You may see something. You may not. You may hear something. You may not. No matter what does or does not happen, you will know you have been activated, energized, and renewed. How will you know? Trust me, you will know, and the evidence will not be the same for everyone.

I am tempted to give you instructions about how to breathe, how to sit, where to sit. I will resist that temptation because I suspect the instructions will confuse you into thinking there is a right way and a wrong way. There are those who will tell you to focus on a word. For some, that is a good place to start. Others will say you should chant aloud or mentally. That also works. In the past, I have said you must breathe deeply, rhythmically, in order to still the mind and access the power of the Divine. I still believe that, and I know it works for me. However, because I believe more in the necessity to meditate than I do in any one correct way to do it, I will say simply *be still and know* there is a universal power seeking an outlet through you. The instrument of this power is your mind. When you still the mind to all outside influences and internal chatter, the power will become activated. *Be still and know* there is nothing more important than the time you spend in the presence of the universal power. For those few moments of the day, people must leave you alone. You must give yourself up and over to the invisible force of life. The results of this stillness, silence, and act of trust will be growth. You will grow in mental ability and spiritual understanding. You will grow in awareness and ability. You will grow in consciousness. You will grow in your divinity.

I do offer you one small suggestion. I suggest that you begin all meditation with prayer. It has been said that prayer is when we talk to the Divine and meditation is when we listen. If we begin by talking to the Divine about what we would like to know, we will receive the appropriate response. Getting a response, however, must not be the goal. We must know that once the need is put forth in the form of a prayer, the response will be forthcoming. It may not come today, but it will come. When we take goals into meditation we run the risk of being disappointed or discouraged. I would also suggest that meditation becomes the primary source of spiritual nourishment in your life. In the same way we feed our bodies three times a day, we should feed our spirit. Just as we would never consider running our car without gas, we should not consider running our lives without the power of the Divine. Think of meditation as a pit stop. You must stop every now and then to check in, making sure all systems are go!

Commentary Journal

After reading today's commentary, I realize

The key phrase(s) I want to remember and work with today are

Morning MEDITATION Affirmation

I know there is only one Life, one Power, one Mind, one Spirit of universal intelligence, wisdom, and judgment. I know this Life, Power, Mind, Spirit is all-knowing, all-powerful, unlimited, abundant, joyous, and peaceful. I know that this presence moves in my being as the true essence of what I am. For this, I am so grateful.

I know that right here and right now the power and presence of the universal Mind, the Spirit of life, is moving through my being, connecting all fragments of thought and emotion into a consistent flow of divine intelligence. I know that right here and right now, the unlimited, healing presence of the Divine Mind is infusing my entire being with its light, its love, its perfection. For this I am so grateful.

I know that right here and now, all that is good, all that is Divine is at my disposal, and that I am willing to be used as a vessel for the Divine to spill forth as goodness, peace, well-being, and love for my own betterment and the betterment of all mankind. I now wipe clean my emotional and mental self in order that I may be filled with the light, love, intelligence, and wisdom of the divine truth of life. For this I am so grateful. And So It Is!

Let Me Remember . . .

MEDITATION is not hard. MEDITATION is necessary.

Everything I need or need to know is available to me in stillness.

When I am still, the power of the Divine is active.

If I want to be activated I must plug in.

In stillness there is knowing.

Evening MEDITATION Journal

I was not able to meditate today because

When I am able to meditate I feel

I believe MEDITATION is necessary/unnecessary because

DAY 5

Honor the Divine
with . . . WILLINGNESS

Working Definition:

The principle we are working with today is WILLINGNESS. It is a state of mental and emotional receptivity. The will is the controlling and directive faculty of the mind that determines consciousness and character. Willingness is a state of consciousness that allows the mental faculty to be infused with the will of the Divine.

Commentary on WILLINGNESS

There have been times when I knew exactly what needed to be done to bring resolution in the midst of conflict, the end to an unbearable situation, clarity at a time of confusion and chaos. I knew what to do, but I was not always willing to do it. More often than not, I was afraid of the outcome. I was not willing to make people angry or hurt their feelings. I was not willing to take the first step, particularly if I could not see where that step would lead, or if I was afraid of where it might lead. I was not willing to sound weird or stupid or like a know-it-all. I was not willing to run the risk of being wrong. I was not willing or prepared to defend myself if I were challenged. Yes, I admit it. I knew what needed to be done, but I was not willing to do it. I was in resistance.

Resistance to doing what we know must be done is a derivative of fear. Fear is a tool of the ego. Fear, cleverly disguised as resistance, supports unwillingness. We are unwilling to be wrong, to look or sound stupid, to be challenged or defeated. The more entrenched we become in resistance, the further we move away from a state of willingness. The Divine does not remember our errors or calculate our perceived defeats. Nor does the divine energy of life judge our methods or choices. The Divine merely asks us to be willing to do whatever is necessary to move into our own state of Divinity, which means that we must develop wisdom, judgment, and courage through willingness.

In many of the experiences we face in life, it is not that we don't know what to do or say. The greatest percentage of the time we don't know how to do or say it. Willingness enables you to say what is required at any given time. It infuses your consciousness with the spirit of love, which will miraculously spill forth from your mouth when you are courageous enough to allow it. At those times when we do know *what* to say and *how* to say it, we cannot figure out *when* or *if* to say it. Willingness ignites the spark of divine judgment that leads you to the portal of perfect timing or silence, whichever you deem to be most appropriate at the time. Speaking for myself, I will say I usually know exactly what to do and how to do it. As a rational, thinking being, I daydream. I imagine. In these imaginative states, I would see and hear myself saying and doing things that I dared not do "in my right mind." This "right mind" was the people-pleasing part of my ego that cut willingness off at the knees. Willingness, I have discovered, fosters and builds a courageous character. We all need the courage in order to be willing to honor the Divine in the face of our human challenges.

Willingness strengthens the connection between the physical mind and the divine or spiritual mind. The outgrowth of this connection is a sound spiritual character. When you are willing to be a true representative of divine energy, you realize the necessity to build a solid spiritual foundation. You know to pray first. You trust that the answer will come forth. You act on what your heart tells you, knowing the Divine always speaks the truth directly into your heart, your feeling nature. When you are willing to build a spiritual foundation, you know you will be protected and guided, and that you will be infused with the light and love of the Divine. This infusion is spiritual in nature, and may show up looking pretty weird on the physical level.

When you are in a state of spiritual willingness, doing or saying what your spirit tells you to do or say, people will not always be happy with you. You, they will think, are being a royal pain in the behind! You, they will accuse, are disturbing the status quo. You, they will attack, are keeping them from having their way. On the other hand, in your state of willingness, you may be the only vessel available to the Divine at any given moment. The Divine always needs a vessel to pour forth Its energy. Mark Twain once said, "You may be the only Bible somebody else reads." If this statement is in fact true, we owe it to ourselves and the Divine to present ourselves as clear, supportive, and encouraging of information. To be a divine Holy Book requires the kind of courage that willingness will develop.

Willingness does not mean that people will agree with you or that things will always go the way you think or feel they should. On the other hand, willingness leads to cooperation. Cooperation demonstrates a willingness to move beyond your way of thinking. When even one person in a situation is willing and able to let go, tension is relieved. Where there is no tension, there is peace. Peace is the energy of the Divine. Willingness does not make your life easier. What it will do, however, is make it easier for you to move through every experience that may confront you in life. Having the courage to speak your mind and tell the truth from a position of love rather than anger or fear, being open to accept the views of others without feeling threatened or defeated, relinquishing the ego's need to be in control by demonstrating the willingness to do whatever it takes to establish peace— all these types of willingness lead to growth. You grow in mental agility, spiritual fortitude, and divine stamina.

Divinely ordered thinking is another outgrowth of true willingness. When you are willing to give up your thoughts to Divine Mind, you receive Divine guidance. This guidance enables you to elevate your feelings to a divine nature: the nature of love, openness, and peace. As your divine nature unfolds, you become willing to do more than pray. You become willing to march in pursuit of those things that are in your best interest and the best interest of the world around you. Willingness is an active declaration that life is a divine game, but it is your move! When you move, you want to be able to make it through difficulties and challenges. Be willing to be wrong. Be willing to walk the extra mile. Be willing to fall down, get up, and fall again, knowing that divine counsel is only a moment of stillness away. Of all the spiritual principles that take us into moments of grace, willingness is one that teaches us that, when we are willing to give up everything we have, the Divine will replace it with ten times more.

Commentary Journal

After reading today's commentary, I realize

The key phrase(s) I want to remember and work with today are

Morning WILLINGNESS Affirmation

I am WILLING to be still.
I am WILLING to trust the Divine presence within me.
I am WILLING to trust the Divine in the stillness of my thoughts.
I am WILLING to trust the Divine with the secrets of my heart.
I am WILLING to trust the Divine with the essence of my life force,
  my spirit.
I am WILLING to hear the voice of the Divine.
I am WILLING to know the will of the Divine.
I am WILLING to surrender myself to the presence of the Divine.
I know that the Divine force of life cares for me, speaks to me, loves me
  `and protects me.
For this I am so grateful!
And So It Is!

Let Me Remember . . .

Thy will, not my will, be done.

I will to will Thy will.

The will of the Divine is my salvation.

To be WILLING is to be courageous.

Evening WILLINGNESS Journal

Today, I discovered the things I was most WILLING to do made me feel

Today, I discovered that when I became resistant I felt

The things I have resisted and now feel ready to do are

DAY
6

Honor the Divine
with . . . CREATIVITY

Working Definition:

The principle we are working with today is CREATIVITY. It is the invisible force behind all things seen. The innate ability of a living element to re-create itself. The spiritual faculty of potentiality. The ability of human beings to bring forth onto the physical/visible level that which is conceived at the mental level (consciously or unconsciously) and the emotional level.

Commentary on CREATIVITY

God couldn't do everything, so the Divine passed on to Its children the same creative ability God has. God actually could have done it all, but if that had been the case, what would be left for you and me to do? Not very much. Instead, the Divine infused us with the power to conceive, express, and enjoy the fruits of our creative power. We create through thought, word, and deed. Although few instructions accompany this ability, it is conceivable that we are each here to reveal the creative ideal of the Divine. This not only translates into artistic creativity; it also refers to our ability to create a world environment that is reflective of divine ideals such as love, peace, abundance, joy, harmony, and power. I think that last one is where we got a bit confused. Instead of using our power to create divinely, we create by default because we do not understand how to use our divine creative power.

Life unfolds from the inside to the outside. I'm not really sure why, and I only think I know how. The how and why really don't matter. It does, just like you and I did. Many have explored the theory of creation and determined that it really does work. Whether we are talking about an apple tree that was planted from a seed or a human being that springs forth from a sperm and an egg, there is a creative principle that brings life from inside darkness to the world of light. I think it is a shame that people spend so much time arguing about the how and why. It is time that could be much better spent teaching people how to use their potential. It's an even bigger shame that intellectuals believe one must be properly trained and guided to develop their creative abilities. God gave every human being the ability to create.

In his *Handbook to Higher Consciousness,* a truly enlightened spiritual teacher named Ken Keyes wrote, *"Your predictions and expectations are . . . self-fulfilling. Since your consciousness (thoughts) create your universe, all you have to do to change your world is to change your consciousness!"* When I first read this, I didn't have a clue! I thought it was some sort of hocus-pocus. Think this thought and WAAA-LA! what you want will appear. Of course, that didn't happen when I focused on winning the lottery. But after reading Shakti Gawain's *Creative Visualization,* Joel Goldsmith's *Invisible Supply,* and Charles Filmore's *Atom-smashing Power of the Mind,* I came to realize and understand myself as a divine and creative being whose every thought is manifested as a tangible physical experience. Unfortunately, the stuff I was creating was a nightmare!

Most of us develop a pattern of thinking and behavior we believe cannot be broken. Our mother did it. Her mother did it. Now we do it. Sometimes we are lucky enough to get parents who say, "Don't make the same mistakes I did!" Usually we don't. We make our own brand of mistakes because, like our mothers and fathers, we have not been taught the creative potential of our thoughts and emotions. Few of us are taught that within our beings are millions of seeds of potential. Our thought patterns and emotional responses germinate those seeds that ultimately grow into experiences. Hey, wait a minute! You mean what we are experiencing in our lives, in the world, today, is a reflection of what we think? You've got it! Now let's take a moment to look around at what we have created.

Generally speaking, there is a lot of hate in our world. Many Blacks hate whites and vice versa. Some straights hate gays. Lots of Republicans hate Liberals. The *real* Southerners hate the fast-talking, smart-ass Northerners. Almost everybody hates the mere mention of O.J. for one reason or another. Some of the hate is born from anger. When people disagree with you, you get mad. When people hurt you, you get mad. When you cannot get someone to see things the way you see them, it is a human tendency to get really, really mad. If you make someone mad, they think they hate you. The truth is they are probably afraid of you.

Fear is born of a lack of understanding, the need to control, and, more important, the absence of love. Christians can't love the Muslims. Muslims can't love the Jews. It's actually not true that they *can't* love each other, it's just real hard to move beyond the labels. Boy! Have we created some angry labels! Punk! Nigger! Bitch! Fag! Kike! Dyke! Spic! Pig! Fatty! Skinny! You tag one of these labels on somebody and they are sure to get mad at you. If you say it aloud, you should probably be afraid. And you know what? You don't even have to say what you are thinking out loud. If you think it hard enough, the object to which your thoughts are directed may hate you or be afraid of you and not be able to explain why. In some cases, people can actually feel what you think about them. That's just how powerful we are.

Thought + Word + Action = Results. That is the creation process. In his book *Conversations with God: An Uncommon Dialogue,* Neale Donald Walsch wrote, *"All creation begins with thought ('Proceeds from the Father'). All creation moves to word ('Ask and you shall receive, speak and it shall be done unto you.'). All creation is fulfilled in deed ('And the Word was made flesh and dwelt among us').* The inherent power of creativity within human beings is never idle. When we are aware of the power, we use it constructively, like using fire to cook. When we are unaware of the power or doubt its existence, that same power becomes as destructive as an arsonist's tool. Every second of our lives we are creating individually and collectively.

Because we are not taught the efficacy of our creative potential, we often wade between belief and disbelief, using the power at times, forgetting its potency at others. We live by default, experiencing the results of what we think but dare not say, of what we say mindlessly that in turn evokes a fearful or unloving response from others, and of what we do in response to what we think someone else is doing or saying. Our thoughts unfold as words. Words inspire action. Action creates the environmental conditions we all experience. Hate, anger, dis-ease, poverty, war, as well as joy, beauty, and the abundance of any good thing are done unto us according to the formula of creativity etched into our DNA by the Divine.

I personally do not want to take responsibility for the fierceness of the IRS, corruption in the government, homelessness in Los Angeles, murder in Detroit, or hunger in Somalia. I can hardly face the fact that I am responsible for not paying the mortgage on time. I am sure we can all find reasons, explanations, excuses outside of ourselves that rationally explain many of the challenges we face in life. Yet, as my spiritual growth and understanding evolves, I cannot evade the fact that *I am made in the image and likeness of the Divine.* I am creative. My mind is linked to the mind of the Divine by virtue of my breath. Mind produces ideas that are crystalized as thoughts. I do get angry, afraid, and sometimes downright hateful in response to limited, ego-based perceptions. I have said and done things in response to these perceptions that, I must admit, have adversely affected my children, my mate, my employees, the driver in front of or behind me. My energy ripples out like a stone dropped in a pond and impacts other people. It is true about me, and it is true about you. It is also true that we have created a pretty ugly world.

There is a very simple correction process that puts our innate creativity to a much better use. Start each day by seeing it the way you would want it to be. See yourself handling every responsibility peacefully and effectively. Trust that even when the results you desire do not show up immediately, they will eventually show up. See yourself moving through the day with a smile on your face and joy in your heart. Since the people around you may not be reading this book, you will have to see them responding to your peace and joy in kind. In those moments when you are caught off guard, made angry or frightened, pray immediately for correction. Remember you are a very creative force! Do not add thought, word, or deed to a destructive situation. Stand there and pray. Call in the light of peace, of love, of the Divine. Use your creativity to honor the Divine by calling forth Its energy in the places it is needed. It will not always be easy, but remember, the more damaging and destructive a person behaves, *the greater is their cry for healing and correction.* Only the Divine can heal or correct. Using you as Its device of creativity, the Divine can transform any situation into a corrective healing experience. Be willing to be used as a creative instrument of divine healing and evolution.

COMMENTARY JOURNAL

After reading today's commentary, I realize

The key phrase(s) I want to remember and work with today are

Morning CREATIVITY Affirmation

I am the CREATIVE power of the Divine at work.
I choose to be an expression of good, of peace, of joy and abundance.
The Divine thinks by means of me.
My thoughts are clear.
The Divine expresses Itself in my heart.
My heart is open to the goodness of life.
The Divine CREATES, heals, restores, and builds through every action I take.
My eyes, ears, hands, and feet are instruments of the Divine.
Today, I rejoice in advance for all the good I am CREATING through right thinking, an open, loving heart, and Divine right action.
For all of this and more, I am so grateful.
And So It Is!

Let Me Remember . . .

The Divine formula of CREATIVITY is

Thought + Word + Deed = Results

Every thought is a CREATIVE tool.

My outer world is a CREATIVE reflection of my inner world.

I can change my mind at any time.

I have the power to consciously choose what I think.

Evening CREATIVITY Journal

What I CREATED in my world today was

What I intend to CREATE in my life tomorrow is

What I intend to CREATE in the world is

DAY 7

Honor the Divine
with . . . PEACEFULNESS

Working Definition:

The principle we are working with today is PEACE. It is an internal state of harmony and tranquillity derived from the awareness of peace. Thought, word, and deed produced in response to a desire to create, promote, or maintain a state of peace.

Commentary on PEACEFULNESS

My friend Joia told me a story about a woman and some birds that gave me great insights on peacefulness. She heard the story from her guru, Swami Chidvilasananda (widely known as Gurumayi), a teacher of the Siddha Yoga tradition.

One day a woman went to the park to meditate. She found a quiet, sunny place, spread her blanket, and sat down. She closed her eyes, breathed deeply, and was prepared to begin an inward exploration of her thoughts and feelings. As her breathing became regulated and her mind still, she became aware of some birds chirping near her. At first it was a melodic and peaceful addition to her inward journey. Within moments, however, the birds began to squawk, almost scream at each other. As the woman tried to stay focused on her breathing, the birds seemed to squawk louder and louder.

The woman's eyes flew open. There were at least twenty birds sitting around her, screeching at each other. She looked around and the rest of the park was empty. Halfheartedly, with a flinging gesture of her hands, the woman shooed the birds away. Some left. Some remained. Those who remained became very quiet, until she closed her eyes.

It seemed as if the second she closed her eyes, the birds started screeching again. Quite annoyed, the woman got up and moved. The birds flew away. Upon finding another prime spot of grass, the woman sat down to begin the process all over again. As soon as she did, the birds came back. "This is ridiculous!" the woman said to the birds. "Shoo! Shoo! Go on! Get out of here!" The birds flew a little higher, but in a seeming act of defiance, they continued to squawk. Totally pissed off with the birds for disturbing her peace, the woman stood up and began to chase the birds. She would run to the left, and fling her blanket at them. The birds would fly away, but they wouldn't shut up. As soon as she cleared those on the left, a new crew arrived to her right. Changing directions, she would shoo them away. They would circle her, squawking, and swoop down a few feet away. Within moments, the woman was flinging her arms around like a lunatic, screaming at the birds who were squawking back at her. Realizing how crazy she must have looked, she snatched her blanket from the ground and stormed out of the park.

Later that evening the woman had an opportunity to relate her experience in the park to her guru, her teacher. Her exasperation returned even in the midst of telling the story. The guru smiled and asked, "Why did you not welcome them to join you?" "How was I supposed to do that?" she asked. "Om Nama Shiva," the Guru responded, "which means, 'I surrender to Shiva (meaning the God) within me.' "

A few days later the woman went back to the park. She went through the entire process again. The moment she became still, the birds began to sing. As soon as she heard them, she mentally affirmed, "Om Nama Shiva." The birds began to squawk. "Om Nama Shiva." It began to sound as if every bird in the state had converged on the very spot where she was sitting. She never opened her eyes. She continued to breathe deeply, affirming louder and louder in her mind, "Om Nama Shiva. Om Nama Shiva! OM NAMA SHIVA!" She thought the words faster and louder. So fast and loud in fact that she became so mentally exhilarated that she stopped. It was then that she noticed the silence. Either the birds had flown away or simply shut up. She did not open her eyes to determine which had occurred.

Why is it that we will walk into a room of screaming children and yell at the top of our lungs, "BE QUIET!" If you want peace, be peace. My grandson Oluwa, age five, is afflicted with a common childhood ailment. He cannot speak below 100 decibels. He yells as if he secretly believes that everyone in the room is hard of hearing. One day someone in the family (due to threats of being sued for slander, I cannot reveal who) became so frustrated with him that they yelled, "Will you please be quiet!" Other people present in the room chimed in by screaming, "Thank you!" His silence lasted for about three minutes. His next comment was made at the usual ear-piercing level.

If you want peace, be peaceful. Because I am the wise old granny, I have learned to take a completely different approach. When Oluwa screams at me, I crouch down to his level, put my nose directly up against his nose, smile, and whisper, "I can't hear you. You are talking too loud." He didn't get it at first, but I would stay there, staring at him eyeball to eyeball, until he lowered his voice. Now when Oluwa approaches me, he usually whispers so softly I must ask him to repeat himself. He and everyone else in the family still seem to have a problem hearing one another. I watch them and I smile. If you want to experience peacefulness you must begin from a posture of peace. One word of caution: Be prepared to stay in that posture for as long as it takes.

Commentary Journal

After reading today's commentary, I realize

The key phrase(s) I want to remember and work with today are

Morning PEACEFULNESS Affirmation

I am PEACE, PEACEFULLY expressing myself as PEACEFULNESS.
I am PEACE, PEACEFULLY expressing myself as PEACEFULNESS.
I am PEACE, PEACEFULLY expressing myself as PEACEFULNESS.
I am PEACE, PEACEFULLY expressing myself as PEACEFULNESS.
I am PEACE, PEACEFULLY expressing myself as PEACEFULNESS.
I am PEACE, PEACEFULLY expressing myself as PEACEFULNESS.
I am PEACE, PEACEFULLY expressing myself as PEACEFULNESS.
I am PEACE, PEACEFULLY expressing myself as PEACEFULNESS.
I am PEACE, PEACEFULLY expressing myself as PEACEFULNESS.
Nothing can disturb this expression of PEACEFUL PEACEFULNESS.
Nothing can disturb this expression of PEACEFUL PEACEFULNESS.
Nothing can disturb this expression of PEACEFUL PEACEFULNESS.
Nothing can disturb this expression of PEACEFUL PEACEFULNESS.
Nothing can disturb this expression of PEACEFUL PEACEFULNESS.
Nothing can disturb this expression of PEACEFUL PEACEFULNESS.
Nothing can disturb this expression of PEACEFUL PEACEFULNESS.
Nothing can disturb this expression of PEACEFUL PEACEFULNESS.
Nothing can disturb this expression of PEACEFUL PEACEFULNESS.
PEACE is the order of this day.
PEACE is the order of this day.
PEACE is the order of this day.
As I am, So It Is!
For this I am so grateful!

Let Me Remember . . .

To have peace, I must be PEACEFUL.

I can choose PEACE in all situations.

Nothing in the world can disturb the PEACE I create within.

I welcome others to join me in PEACE.

Today, I realized it is easy to remain PEACEFUL when

I find it is difficult for me to remain PEACEFUL when

As of this moment I am completely at PEACE about

DAY
8

Honor the Divine
with . . . SIMPLICITY

Working Definition:

The principle we are working with today is SIMPLICITY. It is the state of being simple, uncompounded, or uncomplicated. Clear. Direct. Existing in the most basic form. Free of judgment or perception.

Commentary on SIMPLICITY

We love each other. It took thirty years, and three marriages (to other people) for us to reach this conclusion. It resulted in our decision to spend the rest of our lives married to each another. (The entire story is a subject for another book.) In the most simplistic, direct form, this was our story. I am sure the hearts of most women flutter at the very thought of finally being with the one man you have loved all your life. The very thought of it would probably take Madonna's breath away. I'm sure it would be enough even for her. It was not, however, enough for me. I had to have a wedding.

Picture this, if you will: He's forty-six, I'm forty-four. He's got seven children, I've got three. His parents are divorced, his father remarried. My parents are deceased. He's got two ex-wives with whom he maintains very supportive relationships. I've got three best friends (one of whom is my daughter), and we want to have a wedding. Correction. A big wedding. Wait. There's more! It has to be an outdoor wedding (my idea), with a live band (his idea), no tent (too expensive), near a hotel (all of the children, parents, best friends, ex's, and the band members live out of town), on the Saturday before Mother's Day. I would say that was about as complicated as simply being in love and wanting to get married could get. If I said that, however, I would not be telling the truth. He lives in Georgia, I live in Maryland. Wait. There's more.

The astrologer would have to help us pick the date. This date would then have to be checked with the numerologist. I would never forgive myself if on our own we chose a date when the stars and planets were doing something weird. The two "ologists" could not agree. After digesting the information, we picked what promised to be the best of the two dates. Next I designed the invitation. It was an odd-size invitation to be printed on hard-to-find paper, which did not match any of the standard-size envelopes, which many printers looked at and said, "I've never seen anything like this! We *might* be able to do it, but it's going to cost you!"

Next I hired a planner, who immediately asked, "What's the budget?" Budget? What budget? This is what we want, and we need you to help us pull it together. "You must have a budget so that we can negotiate the best price for everything." I gave her a figure off the top of my head. "That's reasonable," she said, as she went out to hunt and gather the things we wanted and needed. How was I to know that, when she mentioned my semi-well-known name to an enterprising business person, business savvy would rise to a whole new level. Or that the new level would create the need for a budgetary adjustment or real hard-bargaining tactics. My planner knew how to drive a hard bargain. Unfortunately, that was of no use to us in obtaining the material for my dress, which was coming from another country to be shipped to a designer who lived in another state. Wait. There's still more.

There was another event scheduled immediately after our wedding. We had four hours to complete the ceremony and the reception. An hour for the ceremony. An hour for pictures. That left two hours to dance, eat, and greet about 300 guests. The thought of it took my breath away. Move the time back an hour. It felt better, but it would require the planner and I working very closely together to come up with a manageable schedule. Under normal circumstances, a bride working with an experienced planner to coordinate a simple wedding would not be a difficult task. In this case, however, I was not planning a simple wedding.

I was planning a wedding at the same time that I was moving a business into a new building that mysteriously developed a leaking roof three days after we moved in. I was planning a wedding at the same time that I was completing not one but two different manuscripts. I was planning a wedding with a maid of honor and matron of honor who lived in Alaska and Detroit, respectively. I was an orphan planning a wedding and trying to decide who should give me away: my twenty-six-year-old son, who insisted he would have to wear sunglasses, my very public-shy godfather, or my older brother, who might or might not decide to show up, despite his semi-sober pronouncement after a ten-year absence, "You know I'll be there!"

I really believe there is something in the human psyche that abhors sim-plicity. There was a time in my life that unless there was a slight bit of drama going on, I became suspicious. I have worked diligently over the years to heal myself of that affliction. Yet, somehow, in my creation of my world, I suffered a relapse. Why didn't I invite his mother and children, my children, and a few friends over to my one-acre backyard to witness my godfather, who is a minister, marrying us? Why didn't my future husband shake me, pinch me, or in some other way negotiate with me to begin our life as a couple in a more tranquil and simplistic way? Why? Because we are all human, and that would have been too simple.

I was riding the bus one day when a woman and I struck up a conversa-tion about mothers. I told her how much I missed mine. She was my inspi-ration and my best friend. I recalled how many times I had picked up the telephone in the face of good or bad news to dial my mother's number. It was usually when I heard the disconnect recording that I would remember she was gone. "What happened to her?" the woman asked. "She died." "I'm sorry for your loss," she continued, "but what happened to her?" "She stopped breathing." I knew where she was going, and I wasn't going there on this bus with a perfect stranger. "I realized she died, but what hap-pened? I mean, was she sick?" The woman was actually displaying signs of annoyance. "Perhaps," I said. "But, in the end, she simply decided to relin-quish her body and its place on the planet, so she just stopped breathing." Now, totally exasperated, she retorted, "Well, that's a pretty simplistic view of your mother's death."

Death, I thought to myself, is simple. Stop breathing. Stop living. Very often, when we create drama in our lives, we stop breathing. We stop think-ing. Our hands become cold. Our senses are dulled. Our mouth becomes dry. It's called stress. More often than not, stress is not induced by situa-tions and circumstances we face. It is an outgrowth of our response to the situation. Human beings crave the complex, dramatic, gory, heart-wrench-ing slant on most things. We have seen evidence of it time and time again, even before the two and a half years of the O.J. production. In fact, that entire production was staged in response to our collective craving. "Keep it simple!" To hear those three simple words once cost me $4,100.00 (perhaps I'll tell that story in another book). I thought I was cured. Obviously I was wrong. Life, however, always provides us with opportunities for self-correction. I am almost sure that my wedding production will do the trick.

After reading today's commentary, I realize

The key phrase(s) I want to remember and work with today are

Morning SIMPLICITY Affirmation

Today, I realize the SIMPLE truth that God loves me.

Today, I acknowledge the SIMPLE truth that I am a creative being, made in the image and the likeness of God.

Today, I realize the SIMPLE truth that I choose my world by what I think, what I say, and what I do.

Today, I understand the SIMPLE truth that there is no need for my life to be difficult. Nor is there any reason for me to lack any good thing. Nor can I be denied what is mine by Divine right.

Today, I accept the SIMPLE truth, that SIMPLE faith , grounded in SIMPLE trust, grounded by SIMPLE prayer, will yield SIMPLY fantastic results!

For the knowledge of these SIMPLE truths I Am so grateful!

And So It Is!

Let Me Remember . . .

God SIMPLY loves me.

Love is not complicated.

Fear complicates all matters.

Willingness and truth lead to SIMPLICITY.

I can choose SIMPLICITY over complication.

Today, I discovered a SIMPLE approach to

Today, I discovered that SIMPLICITY is easily maintained in a situation when

I intend to create a SIMPLER approach to

Phase Two

Honor your own Self.
Meditate on your own Self.
Worship your own Self.
Kneel to your own Self.
Understand your own Self.
Your God dwells within you as you.

MUKTANANDA

Honor Your Self

I did not want to go. There was no particular reason other than the fact that they didn't like me and I wasn't particularly fond of them. There was bad blood between us, bad family blood. Bad family blood means that you do your best to keep the peace even when it means sitting around people, acting like you are comfortable when you are miserable. I'm sure we would all play the "I love you no matter what" game. We all knew how to play the game well. We knew how to smile and exchange niceties to hide the anger or fear that was seething beneath the surface. We all knew which side the other was on even if we would never admit it. It was a bright sunny day, and I did not feel like playing that game. I also knew there was no excuse short of being dead that would be acceptable if I did not go. Instead of getting ready I was trying to figure out how to be dead for just one day.

Where are we taught that it is okay to say what you feel when you feel it? Certainly it is not when we are children. As children we are taught what not to say and what not to do if or when it will make others uncomfortable. The others are the big people. As children we are taught to take care of the big people, the adults, those in authority. Don't talk when the big people are talking. Don't express your ideas if they are different from the big people's ideas. Always accept what the big people offer you, even if you don't like it. In an insidious although not malicious way, we are taught that big people matter and we don't. Even when we become big people ourselves, there are still those who are bigger, older, more important than we are. These are the people we must honor. In honoring the big people, we are taught to dishonor ourselves.

The first way we learn to dishonor ourselves is by not telling the truth. The truth about what we feel, what we want, or what we think. In my family the party lines were, "Children should be seen and not heard!" and, "Nobody asked you!" I've heard others such as, "Be grateful for what you get!" "Don't say that! It's not nice!" When you heard these things you knew to shut your mouth and stuff your feelings because you were treading on very thin ice. If that ice broke you could get yelled at, slapped, or punished. Worse yet, you could get a half-hour-long lecture about the inappropriateness of your behavior. As a child, I learned that spontaneous outbursts of truth about big people, instinctual perceptions about wrongdoings by big people, and clearly observed acts of hypocrisy committed by big people were not to be discussed or challenged. Often I was told not to believe what I saw, or I was convinced that what I felt about a situation was not correct. Instead I was to accept the explanation offered by big people about the situation. As an adult, I continued to view my parents and elder relatives as big people. Eventually this group grew to include employers and other persons in authority. I would do all in my power to honor the feelings and desires of these people, even when it meant dishonoring myself.

When you lie to yourself about what you need, you will eventually lie to others about the same things. I remember that when I started dating I was more concerned with not upsetting my dates than I was with honoring myself. When they showed up late, it was okay. When they did not call as promised, I would question them, but I was very careful not to speak harshly. When they did show up as promised, I had very few opinions about anything. "Where do you want to go?" "Oh, anywhere you choose is fine." "What do you want to eat?" "What do you want?" Answering a question with another question is not a good way to get what you want. It is not the way you honor yourself; however, I was mindful of not asking for too much or not saying the wrong thing, particularly when I had no idea of the kind of budget we were working with. My dates, like my parents, teachers, supervisors, neighbors, ministers, were people who had something that I needed or wanted. I knew better than to offend or upset them. They were big people.

Lying to yourself and other people about what you need, want, like, or do not like is akin to having a bacterial fungus. It spreads quickly into all areas of your life and pollutes your very being. When you are polluted by the fungus of dishonor, it is difficult to speak up for yourself. The fungus seals your lips when people speak to you in inappropriate ways. The fungus clouds your brain when people behave toward you in an inappropriate manner. This lip-sealing, brain-clouding fungus always makes you doubt yourself. It makes you question what you are feeling when you are feeling it. It prohibits your finding the most appropriate way to respond when your sensibilities are offended by big people. But like all bacteria, a fungus that is not treated will turn into an infection. The infection that grows when you do not honor yourself becomes anger or rage. Anger or rage becomes what pours forth from you when big people, or little people, for that matter, say or do things that have gone unchecked by you for long periods of time. The fungus of not honoring what you feel when you feel it, or saying what you need to say when you need to say it, will pour forth as anger and pollute your relationships. Family relationships. Professional relationships. Personal and intimate relationships. None are immune to the fungus that grows within when you do not honor yourself every step of the way, along the way, in your relationships with other people.

I was thirty years old when someone finally told me that I mattered enough for them to care about what I felt. I was standing in a circle of strangers, most of whom were older, wealthier, and much more educated than I was at the time, when someone looked me in the eye and said, "Well, what do you think?" I had been married, given birth to three children, and been divorced when somebody uttered the words to me, "Honor yourself!" Talk about blow your mind! It was not something that I had ever considered. Honor myself! Admit what I feel? Say what I am thinking, out loud, in a room full of big people? Ask for what I want, even if I don't see that it is available in the moment? You have got to be out of your mind!! The person was not insane. He was a minister, and I was in an empowerment workshop. We were going through an exercise designed to develop trust and truth. He had told us that the only way to learn to trust yourself enough to honor yourself as a divine and unique expression of God was to tell the truth. He was in charge. He was a big person. Someone in the group had just offered a very harsh criticism of him and, with no warning, he turned to me and asked, "Well, what do you think?" It's really rather hard to think when your brain is frying and your hair is falling off!

"Well . . ." "No wells!" he yelled at me. "The minute you say 'well' or 'I don't know' you are saying you don't want to talk about it! You are here to talk. So talk. What do you think about what she just said?" I could feel the fifty eyeballs in the room piercing my skin. I could hear my grandmother's voice in the background: "If you don't have anything good to say, don't say anything at all." I could see my mother's eyes darting across the room at me, giving me the mother's look that let you know if you opened your mouth you would be swiftly put to death. I could smell my brain matter frying. With all of this going on, there was the big person standing there, waiting for an answer. The words escaped from my mouth before I could examine or censor them. "I feel the same way. I don't think you have to yell and scream at us to get your point across. We are not deaf. We have paid to be here, which means we are willing to learn. It is hard to learn when you are in fear." "Are you really afraid of me?" he asked gently. "No, not really. I think I am more afraid of what you will say or do if I don't give you the right answer." "What is the right answer?" He was pushing it a bit, but it felt good. "I feel like the right answer is the one that pops into your mind at the moment. The big question is, how do you give that answer without hurting or offending the other person?" He got down on his knees, looked me directly in the eye, and said, "Honor what you feel by saying it the way you would want to hear it. When you say it honestly and with love, your job is over."

I did not go to the dinner. I stayed home, puttering around the house. I opened all the windows to let the fresh spring air in. I gave myself a facial and polished my nails. I went out hunting for shoes. When I didn't find any, I bought ice cream instead. When I arrived back at home, I took a nap and had a nightmare. I heard my aunt and grandmother screaming at me for not coming to the dinner. I heard them say how I thought I was better than everyone else and how things always had to go my way. I heard my brother asking me repeatedly why was I so stupid? Didn't I know the way they were? How come I always had to keep things in an uproar? Then my god-sister walked up to me and asked what I was doing there. She told me I should have stayed away, and said my coming would only cause trouble. In the dream, everyone was screaming at me. I could feel their anger, which made me both sad and angry. I screamed back. As usual, they could not hear me because the fungus of anger had clogged all of our ears. I woke up crying, with my heart pounding.

Sitting on the edge of the bed, blowing my nose, I was a little girl again. Trying to please everyone again. Dishonoring myself again. I couldn't figure out which felt worse, not pleasing the big people or dishonoring what I felt. The phone rang. It was my aunt. Without even saying hello, she asked, "What happened to you today?" The dead air of no response encouraged her to rephrase the question: "I mean, we thought something happened to you. Where were you?" Honor yourself! "The day just got away from me." That was not the truth. "And I really did not feel like coming." "Oh, I see. You had something more important to do, I suppose." "No, I just decided to honor what I was feeling, by staying home and taking care of me today." "Boy!" she said. "I really need you to teach me how to do that! I didn't feel like going either, but you know how they are . . ." As I listened to her recount the day, who wore what, who said what, who drank how much, and what they said and did as a result, I smiled and mentally affirmed, "Honor yourself!" It is really a great deal easier than we think.

DAY 9

Honor Your Self
with . . . AWARENESS

Working Definition:

The principle we are working with today is AWARENESS. It is intuitive knowledge. The ability to recognize and harness the spirit of truth in action. Knowledge or information void of emotional charge or judgment.

Commentary on AWARENESS

A teacher once told me, "If one person says you are a horse, you don't have to listen. If two people say you are a horse, you probably need to pay a bit more attention to what you are doing. If three people say you are a horse, more than likely you have hay hanging out of your mouth and a saddle on your back!" In other words, people looking at you can see things that you may not be aware of. Very often we are unwilling or unable to discuss with one another the unpleasant aspects of ourselves. Rather than discuss what we feel, we criticize one another. People always told me I looked angry. When they were not saying I looked angry, they were saying that I was defensive and combative. Whenever these things were said to me, I would become offended and would go into a long tirade about people not knowing me, what I thought, or what I felt. I usually ended my little speech by saying how sick and tired I was of being criticized, and that I was not angry, damn it!

When you refuse to pay attention to what life is saying to you, life will make its point very clear. Life wants us to be aware of ourselves so we can make the necessary adjustments in order to live more harmoniously. Life was trying to make me aware that I was acting like a horse, but I kept insisting that I was a kitten. Life was trying to remind me that I was a divine representative of God acting like a complete fool. One day, it became very clear that I had hay hanging out of my mouth.

A friend of mine needed some help in getting some paperwork through an administrative bureaucracy. As an administrator in the institution, I had a few favors to call in, so I accompanied her to the office of the woman who was presenting the problem. When we entered the office, the woman was engaged in a verbal debate with another person. We stood quietly at the counter waiting for our turn to talk to her. Suddenly, and without warning, the woman turned to us and started screaming about what she would and would not do. She then pointed her finger in my face and challenged me to get out of her office. I asked her what her problem was and why she thought she had the right to talk to me in that manner. More words of a very unkind and unprofessional manner were exchanged, and I eventually left the office without resolving the situation.

Two days later, I was sitting at my desk when my supervisor called asking me to report to his office. I arrived to find my supervisor and two other men waiting for me. One of the men handed me a piece of paper. It was an arrest warrant. I was being charged with the felonious assault of the woman with whom I had had the argument two days earlier. The warrant charged that I pushed her across the office, necessitating that she lock herself in the closet to get away from my attack. Next she stated that I waited for her in the parking lot, jumped from behind her parked car, and beat her about the head and face, causing serious injury to her neck and back. She also alleged that I had slashed the tires of her car. The men, who were police officers, said that I would have to appear in court to answer the charges. My supervisor asked what had happened. I recounted the events of that day as best I could, assuring him that I had not seen the woman once I left the office. I told him I did not know what kind of car she drove and, since I did not have a car, it was unlikely that I would be lurking around in the parking lot. Witnesses. What about witnesses? There were none, but the woman had identified me by name.

Being accused of doing something you did not do is one thing. Being charged with a crime you did not commit is a completely different story. It is a horror story! I went back to the woman's office in an attempt to figure out what was going on. When I walked in, people started shuffling papers around on their desks. In other words, they were ignoring me. Asking no one in particular, I said, who in the office saw me push this woman? No one responded. Then I asked them to show me the closet. There was only a supply closet that contained six shelves. Where did she hide? I asked. Still no response. I knew these people. We had worked together for years. Were they losing their minds? Or had I lost my mind, blacked out, and attacked this woman? I kept questioning myself and other people. Nobody had any clues about what was really going on.

Over the course of the next several weeks, the horror story became a nightmare. The woman came back to work wearing a neck brace. She was suing the institution, which was liable for the actions of its administrative staff. There were stories and pictures printed in the local newspaper. People who had known me for years stopped speaking to me, including the woman who had asked for my help. I was moved from my nice cushy office to an office in the warehouse building. I was questioned repeatedly by the police, the board of directors, and the corporation attorneys. The most amazing thing was, with absolutely no evidence to substantiate her claims, most of the people I spoke to believed my accuser.

Life was obviously trying to tell me something, but in my fear and anger I was rendered deaf, dumb, and blind. Okay, so maybe I had stormed out of a few meetings. And so what if I had fired five or six secretaries in the past year? None of this meant that I went around beating people up in parking lots. What it did mean, however, was that I was totally unaware of how people saw and responded to me. My supervisor's assistant stopped by my office one day just to chat. Eventually we got around to discussing the charges against me. I told her how hard it was for me to understand why people believed this woman. She told me, "That's just how people see you. They see you as angry and threatening. People are intimidated by you. I know your bark is worse than your bite, and I know that you are not guilty. But other people believe that what she says is quite possible." Don't you just love people who come right out and say what's on their mind? Isn't it even more thrilling when what they say shuts your mouth and sits you down? I wanted to say I had no idea what she was talking about, but that would not have been true. I knew.

My supervisor once told me that all I had to do was walk into the room and trouble followed me. Why? Why would he say that? More important, why was it true? Someone else said there was something about me that left a bad taste in people's mouths. These statements, usually made in the form of criticism, kept me on the defensive. Criticism, when offered in a way that invalidates you, will do that. If, however, you are on the path to self-aware-ness and personal growth, criticism can provide you with very profound insights into yourself. If you can move beyond anger and fear, those who criticize you are actually using the only means they know of to make you aware of how you impact the world. If you can control the ego long enough to hear what is being said, you may just realize that people usually say to you the very things you have said silently to yourself.

The charges were eventually dropped, and it was many years later before any of it made any sense to me. It made no sense at all until I stabbed my husband, crashed my car, and had a nervous breakdown. It was anger. It was fear. It was this series of events that made me aware of how aggressive and combative I could be in response to anger. If you have ever been really angry with someone, you know how hard it can be to feel good about that person. The mere thought of them can send you into a rage. If you can imagine the impact of this degree of anger being directed at someone, imagine the impact it has when it is directed at the person you see in the mirror every morning! People know when you are angry. They sense it in your voice. They see it in your mannerisms. People respond to anger with fear. Fear can make a person see something that is not there, or hear something that is not said. This is what I had experienced. The energy inside me, of which I was totally unaware, had manifested as an experience of anger and fear.

Becoming aware of yourself and the impact you have on the world is not an easy task. It is not for the faint of heart or the weak in mind. It requires the same kind of determination I imagine most Olympic distance runners must have. You must be willing to listen, keep plugging away learning to accept, understand, and love yourself exactly as you are, coming from where you have been. The first step toward awareness is being willing to look at yourself and your life without judgment or self-criticism. Every little detail must be examined. Every experience, incident, and entanglement must be revisited and explored. It was James Baldwin who said, "You cannot fix what you will not face!" The clue to successful awareness is that you only have to *look* and become *aware,* you do not *have to fix.* Once you are aware, you are empowered to choose what works and what does not work. Once you become aware, there is no longer a need to fear criticism. You realize that people are not trying to invalidate who you are or what you do. When folks point out unpleasant things about you of which you are already aware, rather than falling into the trap of anger, you can simply say, "Thank you for sharing. I know that about myself, and I am working on it!"

Commentary Journal

After reading today's commentary, I realize

The key phrase(s) I want to remember and work with today are

Morning AWARENESS Affirmation

Today, I choose AWARENESS.
I choose to be AWARE of the beauty of life and living.
I choose to be AWARE of the simple truths in life.
I choose to be AWARE of the simple pleasures in life.
I choose AWARENESS of joy.
I choose AWARENESS of peace.
I choose AWARENESS of love.
I choose to see, to feel, to know, the presence of divine energy in myself and those around me.
Today, I choose to be AWARE and to embrace all that is good, noble, and divine.
As my AWARENESS of joy, peace, love, and goodness grow in my consciousness, joy, peace, love, and goodness become the reality in which I live.
For this I am so grateful!
And So It Is!

Let Me Remember . . .

Life always makes me AWARE of what I need to know.

I cannot change what I am not willing to face.

AWARENESS is the path to better choices.

Self-AWARENESS is the key to peace.

AWARENESS opens the mind and heart to new possibilities.

Evening AWARENESS Journal

Today, I became AWARE of the impact on me when

Today, I realized I am not always AWARE of

I am now AWARE that I can have the greatest impact on others when

DAY
10

Honor Your Self
with . . . ACCEPTANCE

Working Definition:

The principle we are working with today is ACCEPTANCE. It is receiving without criticism or judgment. To embrace the fullness of a situation or experience. An inner realization that all is well, regardless of the outward expression.

Commentary on ACCEPTANCE

I knew my husband was sleeping around, but I could not, would not, accept it. To accept it meant I would have to do something about it, and I did not know what to do. I had no job and no money, so I could not leave him. I had three children who adored their father, and I would not deny them the pleasure of his company. On top of it all, I had a rip-roaring inferiority complex, and I was not going to give "my man" up to another woman. Although I felt unworthy, unattractive, and undesirable, I would not accept that my seven-year marriage could be brought to an abrupt halt by the mere presence of a woman. I would hunt her down and kill her. That would be the end of it.

You do not have to like what is going on in your life, but you must accept that *it*, whatever *it* is, is going on. As long as you do not accept reality, you are powerless to define the role you will play. Failure to accept reality is a denial of your power to make a conscious choice. When you do not choose, you live by default. You are a victim of circumstances. This probably sounds very right and makes a great deal of sense. When, however, you discover that something in your life is not going the way you would like it to go, nothing makes sense. It makes you angry or afraid. When you are angry, nothing makes sense. If you are afraid, it makes even less sense. If you are angry, afraid, and planning murder, you *have* no sense. There comes a time in everyone's life when they must accept that nothing makes sense, and they have no sense, but everything will still turn out okay. Acceptance is knowing that no matter what, everything *is* and *will be* just fine.

Acceptance is simply recognition. When you recognize a thing, you see it for what it is. All of our experiences, no matter how awful they appear to be, are temporary. Acceptance of an experience as a temporary situation can make it a lot easier to handle. It does not mean you will not be temporarily angry, frightened, or senseless. It means you can usually handle something in a calmer manner when you know it is a temporary situation. Acceptance is also an express ticket out of fear and anger. It takes you from where you are to where you want to be without stopping in every little hick town of negative emotion. Accepting a thing does not mean you approve of what is going on. Nor does it mean you are not being impacted by what is going on. Acceptance means you are able to withdraw the emotional attachment just long enough to really see what is happening. Without the emotional charge, you may even discover that what is happening has nothing to do with you. You see it, feel it, and may even know that something must be done; however, it is only from the emotionally detached posture of acceptance that you can make a wise choice.

When the woman showed up on my doorstep, I was forced to accept reality. Acceptance is a form of initiation. It is a rite of passage. You are passing from the fantasy you have created in your own mind, for your own protection, into the real world of truth and facts. When you undergo the initiation of acceptance, it usually means that something secret and hidden is being revealed to you. It means you are being called to show what you are made of. You are put on notice that the time has come for you to demonstrate what you stand for. It is an act of courage. Acceptance is the courageous act of doing what you know you must do before you are forced to do it. I asked the woman to come in.

Acceptance is the essence of respect for one's self and others. When you accept the reality of your life, thereby demonstrating your willingness to make a conscious choice, you honor the wisdom, strength, and tenacity of the divine spirit within you. When you accept the reality of the choices others have made, realizing, although you may not like what is going on, that you have the strength and the courage to live through it, you honor the right of others to choose without blaming them for your wounds. You don't like ants at your picnic, but you don't turn the entire park over to them, do you? You accept that the ants have just as much right to be in the park as you do, and you take the necessary precautions to keep them out of your potato salad. Acceptance is like knowing there will be ants at the picnic. It is acknowledgment that there are needs and circumstances other than your own. By making this acknowledgment you are empowered to develop a strategy for your protection without stepping on the needs of others. After she demanded that I give my husband a divorce, I told her the only way she could have him was if she also took his dog.

Without the emotional charge of anger, fear, and victimization, it is easy to accept the reality of your life. By accepting what is, you become keenly aware of what isn't. When you know what isn't, you can begin to determine what you must do. Acceptance also requires a great deal of trust, and even more patience. You must trust yourself enough to know that you will make the right choices. You must trust that the universe will provide you with every single thing you need in order to accomplish what you set out to do. You must accept that what you want to do may not be an easy task, which means you must be patient with yourself. Be patient when you get angry or afraid. Be patient when you are tempted to lie to yourself and not accept the truth. Be patient when it seems things are not going right and may never be right again. Accept that what is yours will come to you in the right way at just the right moment. Patiently acknowledge and accept that what is not for you is not for you, no matter what you choose to tell yourself. Ants do not get discouraged when they climb onto the picnic table, only to discover that all your goodies are covered with aluminum foil. They crawl back down and patiently wait around the table legs until you drop your plate. When the woman left with the six garbage bags full of clothes and the dog, I went out in the backyard and finished hanging the laundry. When there was only one sheet left in the laundry basket, I sat down on the grass and cried.

Commentary Journal

After reading today's commentary, I realize

The key phrase(s) I want to remember and work with today are

Morning ACCEPTANCE Affirmation

I ACCEPT *the presence of divine life expressing itself as me.*
I ACCEPT *my right to be alive.*
I ACCEPT *my right to know joy.*
I ACCEPT *my right to live in peace.*
I ACCEPT *my right to know love, give love, and receive love.*
I ACCEPT *that when I do not choose joy, peace, and love as the founda-*
  tion of my life, I am choosing a reality that is not divine.
Above all, I choose to ACCEPT *the will, joy, peace, and love of the Divine*
  as the center of my being and the foundation of my life.
For this I am so grateful!
And So It Is!

Let Me Remember . . .

ACCEPTANCE is a sign of courage.

ACCEPTANCE empowers me to make a conscious choice.

ACCEPTANCE of what is does not mean liking it as it is.

Choosing in fear is not ACCEPTANCE.

Choosing in anger is not ACCEPTANCE.

ACCEPTANCE requires that I trust myself and the Divine.

ACCEPTANCE requires that I be patient
with myself, others, and the process of life.

Evening ACCEPTANCE Journal

Today, I realized that I resist ACCEPTING reality when

Today, I was able to ACCEPT that I

I am now willing to ACCEPT that_____is/is not

DAY
11

Honor Your Self
with . . . AFFIRMATION

Working Definition:

The principle we are working with today is AFFIRMATION. It is holding steadfast in mind or speaking aloud a statement of truth. A statement made to claim and appropriate that which is truth.

Commentary on AFFIRMATION

Whatever you say to yourself today, let it be something good. Tell yourself you look nice or smell good. Identify your good features and compliment yourself. If you don't believe there is anything about you worth complimenting, repeat a compliment someone else has given you. You must make a habit of beginning each day by telling yourself nice things. Whatever you think about yourself today, let it be something that makes you feel good. Remember all the victories you have had. Remind yourself of the good things, nice things you have done for other people. Remember a time when you experienced love or joy or pride about an accomplishment. It is absolutely necessary to flood your mind with positive thoughts about yourself.

Among all of the duties and responsibilities you must fulfill today, take a few moments to do something for yourself. Buy yourself a little gift. Offer a prayer for yourself. Hug yourself. Spend a few moments listening to your thoughts, repeating self-affirming thoughts or words and weeding out the negative chatter that frequently races through the mind. You are worth five minutes, three times a day. You are like a plant that needs watering to stay alive. Thinking good thoughts about yourself, speaking pleasant words to and for yourself, are like watering a thirsty plant. These are the steps you can take and must take as often as possible to affirm yourself.

Most of us spend the majority of our lives mentally repeating the criticisms and judgments we have heard about ourselves. The subconscious mind is so powerful, it keeps track of every word we have ever heard. People who have spoken to us in anger, in fear, or as a result of their own pain and ignorance leave lasting impressions on our subconscious minds. These words become thoughts. The thoughts become weeds that have a stranglehold on our self-worth and self-esteem. Your *Self* is divine. Your *Self* is powerful. Your *Self* can never be altered. This is the truth about you. No matter what you have heard or experienced, the truth remains the truth. Your job in life is to know the truth and to affirm it as often as possible.

Poet Maya Angelou once talked about the power of words. She said that words are like little energy pellets that shoot forth into the invisible realm of life. Although we cannot see the words, she said, words become the energy that fills a room, home, environment, and our minds. Ms. Angelou described how words stick to the walls, the furniture, the curtains, and our clothing. She believes the words in our environment seep into our being and become a part of who we are. When I reflect on the negative words I have heard about myself and the years I have spent in battle with them, this makes perfectly good sense to me. Words are so very important to our life. The written and spoken word determines what we do in life and how we do it. And, since words ultimately guide our actions, it is important for us to speak words of truth, love, and every good thing we desire to experience into existence. Self-affirming words and actions are necessary to counteract the unpleasant things we have heard about ourselves.

I was born early. So early, in fact, I did not make it to be born in the hospital. I was born in a taxicab. The cab driver was furious. He sued my parents for the cost of cleaning the taxicab. I heard this story at least a thousand times in my life. The story eventually grew to include statements such as, "She's always been a problem!" "She's always been too fast for her own good!" "You've got to watch her because you never know what she might do!" The words, spoken at times when I was being a rambunctious two-year-old or an inquisitive five-year-old or a hormone-driven teenager, were translated into negative self-chatter. The results—I have been chronically late to everything. I was always late for work. I was late for my wedding. I paid my bills late. I liked to eat late at night. I waited until the last possible minute to do any and everything, and usually ended up being late. My work as an attorney healed me of lateness.

When someone is sitting in jail waiting for you to file a motion, you cannot be late. When a judge has the authority to hold you in contempt, which could mean going to jail, you better not be late. When someone is paying you to do something and their freedom or constitutional rights being upheld hinge on you doing it, you simply cannot be late. There is no excuse for being late. The sun is never late. The moon is never late. Spring follows winter every year. You may not know exactly when it is coming, but you know it will show up before December. These divine activities always show up on time. Lateness is so much more than missing a bus or being caught in traffic. It is a silent expression of not honoring your divinity or the divinity of others.

Sixteen years ago, I took off my watch. I began affirming, "Divine timing and divine order guide me in everything I do. I deserve to be on time. I am on time all the time." I wrote this affirmation out on notes. I placed them all around my house and in my car. I stuck one on my wrist, where my watch would have been. Since I never knew what time it was, I could not miscalculate how long it would take me to get dressed or travel to anywhere. I am one of the people who thought it took only ten minutes to get anywhere from everywhere. My goal became to start out early enough to get anywhere in the world on time. It took me about ten years to get it down to a science. There are many times when I am still late. What I have discovered about those situations is that when I am doing something I do not want to do, I show up late. When I have a fear about the possible outcome of a situation, I show up late. When I have not affirmed myself and honored myself for the day, I will be late.

Commentary Journal

After reading today's commentary, I realize

The key phrase(s) I want to remember and work with today are

Morning AFFIRMATION Affirmation

I am a divine instrument of universal power!
I am a divine reflection of universal love!
I am perfection at its best!
I am whole and complete!
I am unlimited and abundant!
I am divinely capable!
I am a beauty to behold!
I am joy in motion!
I am the greatest miracle in the world!
I am the light of the world!
I am all that I am, and life is graced by my presence.
For this I am so grateful!
And So It Is!

Let Me Remember . . .

I am the light of the world.

I am an instrument of the Divine.

I am the greatest miracle in the world.

The truth of who I am cannot be altered or changed.

The way I treat myself determines how others will treat me.

Evening AFFIRMATION Journal

The negative self-talk I heard today was

It is difficult for me to think good thoughts about myself when

The good things I know about myself are

Honor Your Self
with . . . CHOICE

Working Definition:

The principle we are working with today is CHOICE. It is the ability to recognize alternatives and possible consequences, thereby enabling the selection of that which is most desirable, admirable, and honorable. The ability to act in response to the recognized alternatives.

Commentary on CHOICE

There is a wonderful fable about a rabbit and a witch that teaches us about the power of choice. The witch and the rabbit lived in the woods together. They spent many days talking and walking the many wooded trails together. One day, the witch asked the rabbit to come with her to another town. Rabbit did not want to go, but he did not say anything. He walked alongside the witch, talking as if everything was fine. After walking for quite some time, they stopped to rest. Rabbit said, "I'm so thirsty." The witch plucked a leaf from the tree, blew on it, and presented rabbit with a gourd full of water. Rabbit took the gourd, drank the water, and didn't say anything. They continued their journey. During another rest period, the rabbit announced to the witch, "I'm hungry." The witch picked up a stone, blew on it, and turned it into a bunch of radishes. Rabbit accepted the radishes, ate them, and didn't say anything. They continued on their journey. A short while later, the rabbit somehow lost his footing and tumbled down the mountainside into a very deep cavern. The witch changed herself into a bird and flew to the rabbit's side. He was in pretty bad shape. The witch turned herself back into a person. She gathered every leaf and stone she could find. With a few magic words, she made a magic salve that she rubbed all over the rabbit. He lay there for a while. Witch never left his side. Several days later, when rabbit was feeling better, the witch changed herself into an eagle, swooped the rabbit up, and flew away with him. She carried him back to his nest and flew away again.

Many days passed, and the witch had not seen the rabbit. She called for him. She searched for him. She could not find her friend. One day, purely by accident, the witch bumped into the rabbit in the forest. "Why have you been hiding from me? Why didn't you let me know you were doing better?" "Get away from me!" the rabbit screamed. "I'm afraid of you. I don't like you, or the magic things that you do!" The witch was very hurt. Tears were welling up in her eyes as she said to the rabbit, "I helped you because I thought you were my friend. You accepted my magic gifts as if you were my friend. Now you turn on me! Don't you know that I can destroy you! I will not do it because I have been your friend. What I will do is put a curse on you. From this day forth, when you do not make your wishes known, you will lose your power to wish. And when you have no wishes and become afraid, that of which you are afraid will come upon you." The moral of the story is that which you do not choose will choose you, and that which you fear will find you.

It's not that we do not realize that we must make choices; for most of us it is the fear of making the wrong choice. In some cases, the failure to choose is the result of the fear of letting go of the old for the new, the familiar for the unfamiliar. This is the essence of choice: the ability to make our wishes known, to let go and stand on new and unfamiliar ground. What we do not realize is that choice is a divine teacher, for when we choose we learn that nothing is ever put in our path without a reason. When we choose to follow a certain path or engage in a certain activity, it is because that choice holds a lesson for us. When we stand still, refusing to choose, we miss the divine opportunity to develop our intuition and obey the whisperings of our heart. Choice teaches us how to listen, and why we must obey.

The consequences of our choices or our failure to choose teaches us how to live in harmony with our Self. That Self is always guiding and protecting us. It is up to us to choose to listen to what the Self is saying. It speaks to us as feelings. It speaks to us as the need to grow. When the pace of life or nervous habits force us to choose, we may not take time to listen within, weigh all the possible alternatives, and evaluate the consequences. Undoubtedly, these forced choices teach us what works and what does not work in our lives. On the other hand, clearly focused choices, grounded in self-awareness and trust, reveal to you the truth of your inner knowing. Your choices become your personal library of victory and success, or the need to spend more time honoring your self. All choices, whether forced or focused, resistant or courageous, will take you to a level of understanding that will ultimately affect the way you view life.

The willingness to make conscious choices is another way of demonstrating that you are ready to find new ways of living and being before you are forced to do it. When what we do, how we do it, and the way we do it no longer fits our purpose in life, we must choose to do something else. It means we are aware of our patterns, and no longer choose to embrace them. This becomes the choice to grow. When we consciously choose growth over stagnation and fear, the divine spirit of the universe will support our decision by bringing our lesson gently and lovingly. You know that what you imagine is usually far worse than the truth. Consequently when you choose to know the truth, the truth about your strength, your power, your ability to withstand the consequences of your choices, it is never as bad as you imagine it will be. Choice makes it easier, because once you choose and see that things are getting a bit out of hand, or that you are in fact not ready, you have the ability, right, and power to make another choice.

After reading today's commentary, I realize

The key phrase(s) I want to remember and work with today are

Morning CHOICE Affirmation

There is only one Power and one Presence operating in my mind, my body, and all of my life's affairs.

This is the all-encompassing power of the Divine. The power and presence of God.

God's truth, God's peace, God's wisdom, God's joy now fills every aspect of my being.

God's truth is revealed as every CHOICE I make.

God's peace is revealed as every CHOICE I make.

God's wisdom is revealed as every CHOICE I make.

God's love sustains me in every CHOICE I make.

For this I am so grateful!

And So It Is!

Let Me Remember . . .

CHOICE is my divine teacher.

My CHOICES are sustained by divine wisdom.

Silence is a CHOICE not to choose.

Unconscious CHOICE wins by default.

What I resist will persist.

Conscious CHOICE is the path to personal power.

Evening CHOICE Journal

Today, I realized it is difficult for me to make a CHOICE when

Today, I realized it is easy for me to make a CHOICE when

Today, I realized I have not made a conscious CHOICE about

DAY 13

Honor Your Self
with . . . CONSERVATION

Working Definition:

The principle we are working with today is CONSERVATION. It is a state of mindful relaxation. Preservation and protection of resources.

Commentary on CONSERVATION

I think it was my grandmother who made me think I had to stay busy all of the time. Idleness, she told me, was a sign of laziness, and laziness was a sin. It was much later in life that I learned "sin" is an acronym for "*self-inflicted nonsense*." By then it was too late! I had worked myself into a frenzy. I was a busy little bee, flitting around doing a little bit of this and a little bit of that. I was twenty-five years old and I was exhausted. I did not know how to relax. I did not know how to conserve my energy.

Relaxation is the best way to conserve your energy and add years to your life. It begins with rethinking and relearning busy behavior patterns. Are you the first to jump up and clean off the table? Are you the first to say, "I'll help" or "I'll do it!" We got stars for that in first grade. Remember how you raised your hand and begged to clean the board or the erasers? The busy-ness started way back then. We were rewarded for being willing to do more than our share. We were encouraged to stay busy. As a result, we learned to inflict ourselves with self-imposed duties that ultimately lead to mental, physical, and spiritual exhaustion.

Conservation requires a willingness to be still and run the risk of looking lazy. It not only encompasses being physically still; it extends to mental and emotional stillness. In this way, you not only conserve your physical body, you include your mind and spirit as well. You deserve to rest. You have a right to move at a pace that is comfortable. You need time to yourself, for yourself, and with yourself, if you want to remain sane. Constant *busy-ness* can lead to insanity! And this particular type of insanity is always self-inflicted. We learn to measure our importance in life by the number of things we are doing. When we have nothing to do, we feel useless. In the worst-case scenarios, we can believe we are worthless. Self-inflicted worthlessness is a form of insanity.

In much the same way that we have not been taught to conserve ourselves, we missed the lesson in conserving our resources. Time, money, and knowledge are all resources worthy of conserving. Spending your time doing things that do not bring you or anyone pleasure or joy is a waste of a valuable resource. Spending your money in ways and on things that do not benefit you or anyone else is a waste of your resources. Trying to convince people that there is something you know that could be beneficial to them when they are resistant to hearing you is a waste of valuable resources. When we learn the value of who we are and what we have, we become mindful of conservation.

The greatest enemy to the principle of conservation is the fear of being lazy, stingy, and selfish. For some strange reason, we actually believe that to preserve what we have for our own benefit is a bad thing. If you are intelligent, people expect you to share your knowledge. Yet teachers are among the lowest-paid people in society. If you are wealthy, you are expected to give your money to those less fortunate than you. Yes, giving and sharing are wonderful things; however, just because you have several million dollars in the bank does not mean you must find ways to give it away. To close your door, pull down the shades, and spend quiet time alone does not translate into being standoffish or that anything is wrong with you. Conservation begins with honoring your Self enough to spend some time with you away from everyone else. I have been guilty of it myself. I've called rich people greedy when they didn't give what I thought was enough. I've called people selfish for not giving of their time and energy in ways and to causes as I thought they should. I've even called quiet people weird when they were not flitting around. Of course, all of this happened before I learned about the principle and concept of conservation.

Conservation is a form of healing that results in self-awareness, self-forgiveness, and self-esteem. As you learn to conserve your movements, energy, and resources, you learn to heal yourself from destructive behavior patterns. These patterns often lead to the self-inflicted nonsense most closely associated with a false sense of responsibility. Constant *busy-ness* results in the belief that we are responsible for people, circumstances, and situations that may have absolutely nothing to do with our own well-being. Conservation also allows for the healing of our belief system. The things we were taught and experienced as children are the foundation of our beliefs. Many of the beliefs are toxic and self-defeating. More often than not, what we do, how we do it, and why we do it are an outgrowth of these toxic, self-defeating, self-denying experiences. Through conservation of self and resources we learn to heal these wounds. As we do, we become physically, mentally, emotionally, and spiritually sound. This soundness results in our overall growth and evolution. When you are well rested and financially secure, and when you understand the value of your mere presence on the planet, you are able to give more when you do give. Conservation helps you give your best when you are giving, doing, or being.

You don't always have to have something to do. When you do have something to do, do it at a pace that is comfortable. Don't rush. Don't compete. Spend your time in a state of mental, emotional, and spiritual relaxation, knowing that everything always gets done in divine time and according to divine order. Even when your cup of goodness is running over, remember that what is in the cup is yours. Conserve some of your resources for yourself. Grandma said, "Don't spend it all in one place!" A friendly amendment to Granny's wisdom is, don't spend it all, at all. Keep something for a rainy day, and if it never rains in your life, keep it anyway.

The Bible cautions us, "Cast not your pearls before the swine. Neither give what is holy to dogs." Avoid at all costs giving of your knowledge, time, and energy to unworthy causes and people. How do you know if they are unworthy? If you have to fight with people to accept what you are giving them as an act of love, they are not worthy. Trees, rain forests, minerals, and animals are not the only natural resources worthy of our conservation efforts. You are a divinely natural resource. Life wants you to be around a long, long time. Life wants you to be in good shape while you are here. You are no good to life when you are haggard, broke, and broken down. Learning to relax and conserve your natural energies is one of the greatest gifts you can offer life.

Commentary Journal

After reading today's commentary, I realize

The key phrase(s) I want to remember and work with today are

Morning CONSERVATION Affirmation

I rest in Thee. I rest in Thee. I rest in Thee.
All that I am, I rest in Thee.
All that I have, I rest in Thee.
All that I give, I rest in Thee.
All that I do is to Your glory and in Your name.
Teach me to be, to do, to give in ways that honor Your divine presence
in me.
Teach me to CONSERVE my Self, my gifts, my resources, so that I may
always do Your
perfect work.
Guide me in the way that I should go.
Lead me in the perfect path according to Your perfect will for my life.
Give me the wisdom, the ability to discern, and the vision to know Your
will and perform it with grace and ease.
For this I am so grateful!
And So It Is!

Let Me Remember . . .

I am a valuable resource.

CONSERVATION is a process of self-healing.

CONSERVATION builds self-esteem.

CONSERVATION is a necessary stage of personal growth.

I deserve to rest.

What I give to myself, I give to the world.

R-E-L-A-X!

Today, I found it was difficult to relax when

I am aware that I must learn to CONSERVE my time/energy/resources as they relate to

I made progress toward conserving my time/energy/resources today by

Honor Your Self
with . . . Freedom

Working Definition:

The principle we are working with today is FREEDOM. It is the spiritually induced quality or state of being without restraint, bondage, limitation, or repression. A sense of inner and outer well-being.

Commentary on Freedom

Most of my life I thought I wanted money. I believed that if I had money to do what I wanted to do, when I wanted to do it, I would be deliriously happy and free. As a child and as an adult, I have often heard myself say, "Boy! I wish I had a million dollars." I thought that would be my ticket to freedom. One day I woke up with those same thoughts floating around in my mind, and by the end of that day I had $1.1 million. It was a short time later that I realized it was not the money that I actually wanted. My true desire was for the freedom I thought the money would bring. It was too late! I had the money and all of the obligations that came along with earning it.

In his empowerment workshops, author Stuart Wilde asks, "If you are not totally free, ask yourself why?" Why? Because we paint ourselves into boxes that determine what we will allow ourselves to do based on our race, gender, age, and the external expectations that we believe those boxes impart. For the most part, we can go where we want, do what we want, eat, drink, and dress in any way we choose to. Do we choose for ourselves that which we truly desire? Under most of the normal conditions and pressures of life, we do not. We allow labels and expectations to keep us in boxes, then we cry out for freedom. The entire purpose of life on earth is for us to be free, exercise free will, and choose the parameters of our freedom. What do we do? We spend most of our lives doing things and acquiring things that, in many cases, keep us in mental, physical, and emotional bondage.

Freedom is a state of mind. It is the outgrowth of our willingness to make conscious choices of our own free will and to live through the consequences of our choices without blame, shame, or guilt. Freedom is a sign of self-awareness. When you are aware of what it takes to maintain your mental, emotional, and physical well-being and you make conscious choices toward that goal, you are exercising your freedom. Freedom is the recognition of the truth. The truth is that you were created with "designer genes." The genes of the One who created the universe are at the core of your being. You are powerful. You are unlimited. You are the reflection of creative genius. When you realize this truth and accept it as a fact of your reality, you know that you are free to choose whatever you believe to be the truest reflection of your identity. Freedom requires consistent and repeated acts of courage. You must be courageous to admit that all things are possible, and that you are equipped to handle them all. When you are willing to demonstrate this degree of courage and take a risk knowing that, whatever happens, you will land in the exact place where you should be, you are totally and unequivocally free.

I can hear your mind racing out there, about all the things that keep you from being free: your children, money and the lack thereof, laws, rules, responsibilities to others, taxes, etc., etc. Yes. These are realities with which we live each and every day. They affect us in many ways. They do not, however, in any way infringe upon our freedom. FREEDOM IS A STATE OF MIND! What you believe, how you feel, what you do, how you respond to any given circumstance at any given time is the only impediment to freedom. You are always free to choose how you will respond. You are always free to choose what you will do and not do. You are always free to try something new, to take a risk, to challenge the status quo, and to change your mind. That is what freedom is about. It is not about your bank account or level of education. Those things may help you experience a greater freedom of movement and accomplishment. They do not, however, determine whether you are free or not.

Is there racial and gender discrimination? Yes. Is there poverty, disease, and famine? Yes. Is there crime? Yes. Is there social class and social grace bestowed as a result of wealth, heredity, and political clout? You bet there is! And none of it can in any way deny your divine birthright of freedom. The question is, what is it that you want? What is it that you want to do? Are you courageous enough to live the truth of your desires without fear? This is what will determine your freedom. Once you decide what you want and whether you are willing to do what it takes to get it, you are free to follow your dreams. More important, once you are clear about the experience you want to have, you are free to make the choices that will result in your having that experience.

I wanted to be free to travel. I wanted to live in a nice, big house, in a nice ritzy-titsy neighborhood. I wanted the ability to buy the things I wanted, when I wanted them, without concern for the price tag. Those wants had nothing to do with freedom. I was free to travel. I could have been an airline stewardess. I could have joined the Peace Corps. Buying an airline ticket is not the only way you can access travel. In order to be free you must be clear about exactly what it is that you want and be open to any and all possible means of acquiring what you want. Living in a nice, big house means you have to clean it. I do not like housecleaning! How can you be free if you have a big house to clean? Obviously there were some inherent conflicts in my freedom quest.

When you have lots of things, particularly expensive things, there is a deep-seated desire to protect them from harm. This means bars, gates, alarm systems. I didn't want to live behind bars and gates! That's like being in jail! Once again, I discovered evidence of conflict in my search to be free. I think this is true for most of us. The things we think will give us freedom will actually keep us in bondage. What I also discovered is that many of the things I thought I wanted as a demonstration of freedom, I actually wanted for a completely different reason. I wanted things I thought would make me feel better about myself. I had been imprisoned by self-defeating, self-denying attitudes, behaviors, and beliefs.

I got the house, most of the things, and the opportunity to travel long before I got the money. I found freedom about the same time that I turned forty years old. It was then that I was mature enough to examine and peel away any behavior, attitude, or belief that was limiting or restrictive. It was then that I took off my people-pleasing cape. I found freedom about the same time that I developed the courage and the presence of mind to say no without feeling guilty. The immediate outgrowth of my newfound freedom was the ability to ask for what I wanted. This was enhanced by the willingness to ask someone else if the first person said no. My sense of personal freedom increased at the same pace as my willingness to do what felt right to me, even when people said I was crazy. My freedom also kept pace with my willingness to face the thing I feared most. If you can admit you are afraid and keep moving, you will be released from the fear. Freedom from fear, guilt, false responsibilities, and the need to be legitimized by others opens your mind to new choices, new opportunities, and amazing possibilities.

When I realized that God, the divine source of life, not people, was the source and substance of all good things, I was freed from every "ism" that held me captive. When I stopped comparing myself to others, stopped competing with others, when I was able to honestly want the best for everyone, when I became willing to make choices and accept full responsibility for their consequences, every chain that held me in a place of mediocrity and unfulfillment fell away. Speaking for myself, I discovered freedom as an inherent part of my life the day I stopped telling God what I wanted and asked how I could be of service to God. Shortly thereafter, the guidance came, the self-trust deepened, and the gates of my mental, emotional, and spiritual prison flew open. There is something very freeing about knowing that God believes in you.

Commentary Journal

After reading today's commentary, I realize

The key phrase(s) I want to remember and work with today are

Morning FREEDOM Affirmation

Today, I will remember how powerful I am.

Today, I will remember that I am protected, guided, and illuminated by the divine presence in my being.

Today, I will remember the number of times I have been sheltered from the storm.

Today, I will remember that I have been forgiven when I was unable or unwilling to forgive myself.

Today, I will thank the Divine for mercy, grace, and goodness that gives me the FREEDOM to be and grow and live the glory of my divinity.

For this I am so grateful!

And So It Is!

Let Me Remember . . .

God's grace is FREEDOM.

God's perfect and divine plan for my life will set me FREE.

FREEDOM is my divine birthright.

FREEDOM is a state of mind.

I am always FREE to choose.

My FREE will is the foundation of my FREEDOM.

I am FREE to ask for what I want.

FREEDOM is an experience that money cannot buy.

Evening FREEDOM Journal

Today, I realized that my understanding of FREEDOM is

The experience of FREEDOM I seek is

The way in which I have hindered my own FREEDOM is

DAY 15

Honor Your Self with . . . FUN

Working Definition:

The principle we are working with today is joy. FUN is the pursuit of joy. Activities that provide amusement and mental or emotional release.

Commentary on FUN

Do you have toys? In case you have forgotten, toys are things you play with just for the joy of playing. I play with shoes. They are my toys. I go out searching for shoes. When I find them I try them on. Sometimes I buy them, but buying shoes is not playing with shoes. I play with shoes because it is fun. I also play with makeup. I have all types of makeup, and I have been made up at so many cosmetic counters I could have been charged rent. I buy makeup so that I can bring it home and play with it. I have so much fun making up my face that I have spent an entire day doing just that. I used to play with food. I would play with different recipes and make my family eat whatever I cooked. The cooking part was fun, but once food became so expensive, playing with it was a game I had to give up. The point I want to make is that it is absolutely necessary to spend some portion of life having fun.

We can get so caught up in the process of life, the responsibilities of life, what we want from life, that we forget to have fun. Life is a joke. It is absolutely hysterical. If you think about some of the things that go on in life, you would have no choice other than to laugh. Life is a game. Games are intended to be fun, but we work at our games and turn our games into work. We get so caught up in the work portion of life that we forget to play. We forget to have fun. This is where toys can become very helpful. When you commit some time each week to playing and having fun, life gets much easier. When you realize that there is more to life than working and paying bills, when you have something fun to look forward to, life takes on a completely different tone. Fun gives you a new outlook. It helps you expand your mind and your spirit. It keeps you young and vibrant. Fun allows you to think about something other than what you don't have or cannot do and the places you wish you didn't have to go.

Fun is absolutely free. If you don't have toys, you can always get naked. Just take your clothes off and stand in front of the mirror. I guarantee that there will be at least one thing about your body that you can laugh at. If laughing at yourself is too traumatic, laugh at somebody else. I sometimes point and smile at people as I drive by. They are totally shocked. Sometimes they smile back, but more often than not they look around to see who I'm smiling at, knowing it can't be them. We are so serious about life we don't think we should smile at one another, particularly if we don't know one another. I have fun pointing and smiling at people. I have even more fun winking at men. They love it. If you do it just the right way, their face will crack with a big smile. Of course, it's safe because I can pull away when the light turns green.

When was the last time you played dress-up? Or threw a water balloon at someone you know? When was the last time you had a talent show with your children or friends? There are so many simple things we can do to bring joy and laughter into our lives. There are many noncompetitive, non-intellectual things you can do just for the fun of doing them. You can miss the news for one night. You can finish the book tomorrow. The laundry can stay in a neat and orderly pile just a few more hours. Right now, you need to go and have some fun. Go on. Find something fun to do and do it.

After reading today's commentary, I realize

The key phrase(s) I want to remember and work with today are

Morning FUN Affirmation

I know that God is happy when I am happy.
I know that God wants me to be happy all of my life.
I am most happy when I am doing something that I love to do.
I am happy when I am having FUN.
Today, I promise myself that I will find something that I love to do and I
*   will do it just for the fun of it.*
I am so grateful that I can give myself permission to have fun.
And So I Will!

Let Me Remember . . .

God is happy when I am happy.

Life is a game that is meant to be FUN.

There is always time for having FUN.

FUN is the demonstration of the belief in joy.

Today is a FUN day.

The thing that I find the most joy in doing is .

I could not have FUN today because

I have denied myself permission to have FUN because

DAY
16

Honor Yourself
with . . . SURRENDER

Working Definition:

The principle we are working with today is SURRENDER. It is the ability to achieve mental and emotional release. Acknowledgment of the power of spiritual activity. Obedience to spiritual principle, which evolves into an experience of peace and well-being. An act of acceptance.

Commentary on SURRENDER

Have you ever been at home, minding your business, having not washed your body or brushed your teeth, moving slowly so that you won't catch a whiff of yourself in the breeze? It's the kind of thing you might do on a Saturday morning, or on a day you take off from work. There you are, at home, minding your business, not smelling good, when somebody calls you on the telephone and tells you something that sends you into fifth-gear pissosity. It has happened to me. It was completely unexpected. You rarely expect that anyone would call to disturb you when you have not brushed your teeth! It happens. When it does you must be aware that you are being called on to surrender.

There I was minding my own business when the call came in and set my brain to sizzling. The person on the other end of the line told me something that enraged me so, I had to keep shifting the telephone from one ear to another to make sure I didn't go insane. As the words poured forth, the fury grew in my body, so much so that I was pacing, at a very quick pace, in a circle. When I just couldn't stand it anymore, I told the person, "I will be there in the morning, and when I get there this better be straight, otherwise some-body is going to get hurt!" I admit it was not a very spiritual thing to say, but I hadn't brushed my teeth! I hung up the telephone and began to plan the assault. I thought of all the things I would say and do when I got to my desti-nation and confronted the object of my anger. The more I thought about it, the more enraged I became. It didn't help matters when I realized I would have to drive across two states to accomplish the assault. The fact that I would have to put all those miles on my car made bad matters worse!

I wish I could tell you that I have reached the level of spiritual maturity where the day-to-day influences of human existence do not make me angry. If I were to say that I would not be telling the truth. Many people believe that once you embark upon the journey to spirituality, you should not get mad. You should always be loving and understanding. Get a grip! We are human beings! We must also remember the incident when Jesus kicked the table over. I can imagine he told the disciples, "You are really getting on my last nerve!" A spiritual consciousness does not make you immune to nor-mal human response to human experiences. What it does, however, is give you tools to work with. On this particular morning, I needed a tool. As I paced around in a circle like a ravenous beast, I eventually realized that I needed to surrender. I could not say I wasn't angry because I was. I could not say I did not have the desire to hurt someone who had done what I con-sidered to be offensive, because I did. What I could do, did do, was admit that I was angry, and surrender that anger to the presence of the divine energy in me. It was not easy.

It is very dangerous to believe that once you get on the spiritual path, you will be able to see everything that everyone does in a spiritual light. It is foolish to believe that you will always be able to bless your enemy, and think good thoughts about people regardless of what they do. You will not always have the presence of mind to rub your head with crystals, repeat your affirmations, or pray for the good of someone who has angered you. What you can do, however, when rage, fear, or any other negative emotion engulfs your mind and being, is surrender. Admit what you feel. Feel it and then give it up. You must surrender before you engage the influence of the negative. The issue is not that you experience the emotion. The issue is what you do in response to the emotion. When you are on a spiritual jour-ney, surrender is what you must do.

I learned to surrender in the process of buying a home. I realized I had avoided the process because I was afraid of exposing myself to strangers. I was afraid of being judged because I had an *unattractive* credit report. I had convinced myself that no one would give me a mortgage because of my history of financial irresponsibility. When I finally realized that I was afraid to face the questions, the judgments, the rejection I expected to be the result, I had to surrender. I had to admit that I was afraid. I had to allow the fear to work through my brain. I had to feel the rejection, and from that position I had to trust that whatever happened would be good. I had to surrender the shame, the fear, the guilt of exposing my past unconscious deeds to some strange person who had the authority to judge me worthy or unworthy of owning a home. Surrender is the active reminder that there is a divine law in operation, and that we are always accountable to the law. Surrender is an admission that we cannot make anything happen. However, if we are in alignment with the law, we will always get what we deserve. If we are not in alignment, it simply means we must do the work to make ourselves so.

Surrender allows us to face the thing we fear before it becomes a reality. The fear of being wrong. The fear of losing control. The fear of being found out. Most of the time, the thing we fear has absolutely no power, yet we brace ourselves for the worst possibility. In that defensive posture we keep our minds fixed on what could or might happen. The fear of facing that imaginary negative outcome is what keeps us paralyzed. Surrender places us in the offensive position. It gives us the opportunity to plan, and to move according to the plan. When we surrender, we mentally go to the end, through the thing that we fear, which in effect releases fear thoughts from the mind. It helps you realize that no matter what happens, you will be able to handle it. Surrender helps you to become willing to live through the experience, without giving your entire life over to it. It also makes room in your heart and mind for the Divine to give you a new idea. A new thought. When you surrender, give up the fear thoughts, and give up the control of a situation, you open the way for a miracle to take place.

I did not drive across two states to commit a felonious assault. I submitted an application to a mortgage company, and when I was rejected, I made a plan by which I paid off all outstanding debts. There are still certain experiences about which I become angry and frightened, but now I know how to surrender. There is a little prayer I recite when I know I need to surrender. I will share it with you in the hopes that it will bring you as much release as it has brought to me.

Dear God:
At this very moment I find myself in the midst of_____. I know that this is not for my highest and greatest good. I know that this is not a reflec-

tion of your Divine Will. I ask You to remind me how to transform this experience into something that is a reflection of You and my true self. I ask You to fill my heart and mind with Your divine influence, so that I will be in alignment with Your perfect plan for me. I ask You to forgive me for forgetting that I am your beloved child, under Your watchful eye at all times, and that there is nothing outside of You that has any power over me. I forgive myself for allowing this situation the right to exist, and I surrender it to You. Thy will, not my will, be done. And So It Is!

Commentary Journal

After reading today's commentary, I realize

The key phrase(s) I want to remember and work with today are

Morning SURRENDER Affirmation

Today, I SURRENDER.

I lift my hands to Thee.

I acknowledge Divine Presence and Divine Power as the only active force in my life.

I SURRENDER any attachment to outer appearances.

I SURRENDER the toxic emotions of my physical mind to the pure essence of Spirit.

I SURRENDER fear. I SURRENDER shame.

I SURRENDER anger. I SURRENDER resentment.

I SURRENDER control.

I SURRENDER to the Power and Presence that is Divine Will in active motion.

I SURRENDER, knowing Divine Mercy and Divine Grace always work together for my good.

For this I am so grateful!

And So It Is!

Let Me Remember . . .

God is in control.

I cannot make anything happen.

Thy will, not my will, is done in the perfect way at all times.

The Divine Presence in me cannot deny Itself any good thing.

SURRENDER will eliminate fear.

SURRENDER will eliminate anger.

I must be willing to do the work to overcome fear.

Today, I realized I was in fear when

I found it was difficult to SURRENDER what I was feeling because

I found it was easy to SURRENDER when

Phase Three

If you feel you have no faults,
rest assured you have one.
Pride.
If you feel your faults and defects prevent you
from seeing the faults and defects of others,
remember,
You may be the only contact with God someone may have
today.
Be proud of that.

Honor Others

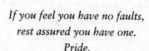

I was crying for my brother. I had done it often before, but today my soul was truly cleansing his pain, grief, and sadness. I have spiritually cleansed for others before, but today it hit me while I was driving at 65 miles an hour on the New Jersey Turnpike. It began when a young man pulled up beside me. Glancing into each others' cars, our eyes met. He had a dark complexion, like my brother. He had the same sparkling, dancing eyes that were my brother's strongest feature when he was young and sober. It was the bald spot that set me off. The same receding hairline that reminded me of my father and my brother all at once. My eyes glazed over, my heart opened up, and I began to cry uncontrollably for my brother.

I was crying because I felt so incredibly inadequate. I had not been able to help him, to save him. He had been drinking and drugging now for about twenty-five years. He seemed angrier than ever. He still wasn't working and now at the age of forty-four, he was facing criminal drug charges. I was a criminal defense attorney, and still I could not help him.

I had watched him for years trying to commit an unconscious form of suicide. I knew he had to know he could not continue doing what he was doing and survive. So many of his friends had already lost their lives to the same despondency that was his modus operandi. It seemed that all of my talking, cajoling, and helping was in vain. When I looked at that young man racing down the road beside me, it became real clear that the only person who could save my brother was my brother himself. That scared the hell out of me.

There's one in every family. A brilliant, free spirit, potentially capable of being the shining star. They usually have some great talent or ability that you can see, and to which they seem completely oblivious. More often than not, they spend most of their time chasing after everything except that at which they are good. The thing right at their fingertips. Those who are closest to them are always fighting off the urge to shake or slap them. You just want to grab them and shake some sense into them. Or perhaps shake some anger out of them. The brilliant ones always seem to be angry or lazy or noncommittal. In some ways, those of us watching know that if they would just get it together, they would not only save themselves, they would probably save us too, not to mention the world around us. We can't figure out what is wrong, and they don't seem to know there is something wrong. Those who do realize they are not fully with it can't seem to figure out how to get with it. It is so frustrating. That is what came over me on the highway—frustration and fear that my brother may never get it together.

I couldn't pull over. I was already late. I had to stay with the pain, the fear, and the tears. In essence, I had to ride it out. In flashback snatches, I saw my brother and I growing up. I saw the abuse hanging from the trees at the side of the road. I saw the neglect on the yellow dividing line that moved ahead of me up the highway. I saw the sadness in my brother's eyes on every exit sign. I heard his crying on the breeze coming in through the slightly open car window. I saw his decision to withdraw into the pain, fear, and anger in the clouds that danced above. I saw my decision to heal in the sunlight that was peaking through the clouds. This was not my pain. It belonged to my brother, and it hung around my neck like a fully packed duffle bag.

What would you have me do, dear God? How can I help him? I turned the radio off in order to hear the answers. My nose was running now. I opened the glove compartment in search of a 7-Eleven napkin. As I reached in, the answer hit me. *"Open yourself to his choices. Honor him by honoring the choices and decisions he has made."* I slammed the glove compartment and let my nose run. What the heck is that supposed to mean? The tears, my nose, the thoughts, I let it all flow naturally. "One of the hardest things we may ever be called to do in life is watch a loved one fall. We want to help them. We want to save them. In doing so, we take away their power and cut off their blessings. What we must do at all times is remember that the God that is loving and helping us is the same God who will help our loved ones when we stay out of the way." Those words from *Lessons in Truth*, by Emilie Cady, raced through my mind, followed by "*God knows what he needs, and the minute he opens himself to receive it, he will. Your job is to pray for his opening and watch for the signs, even the smallest signs that the opening has taken place, the healing is beginning. Honor him enough to know the truth about him. The truth is, God is in the midst of him doing a mighty work.*" I picked up a tissue and blew my nose.

The truth is, I was angry with my brother for not living up to my expectations of his potential. I knew he was brilliant. I knew he was capable, but I couldn't figure out why he couldn't get it together. That made me mad. The truth is, it is very difficult to watch someone we love do bad or suffer. It feels as if they are doing it to us. That makes us angry. The issue is, do we want them to get it together for their sake or our sake? Of course, the natural conclusion is that the answer is a combination. We want the best for them, and we certainly want to feel better about them. There is, however, another truth that often escapes us: People learn what they need to learn the way they choose to learn it, and there is nothing we can do about their choice. The truth is, God hears every prayer. Mine for him. His for himself. It's a good thing that his prayers take precedence over mine. God is wise enough to honor people and their choices, no matter what the choice appears to be.

I guess it is human nature to live vicariously through others. We see ourselves in them, and we only want to see our best attributes in living color. Looking at my brother, I was constantly reminded of my meager beginnings, my family dysfunction, the parental inadequacies that haunted me for most of my life. Having made peace with those experiences in myself, I simply did not want to see them anymore. I resented him showing them to me. There must also be some part of the human psyche that believes what we consider failure is heredity. When we triumph over adversity, we want the confirmation of others through their actions. We want them to make it because we have. If not, there is a tendency to believe that our victory could be short-lived. A freak accident that could end abruptly because of our genetic makeup. Even when we convince ourselves that "they" are the way "they" are because "they" want to be, the fear and anger over their lack of success creates internal conflict. It's not my job to help them! But that's my brother, sister, mother, father! We forget they are also a child of God with complete access to God's grace.

Okay, I admit it. I also felt guilty. "Why me?" I'm not special! We come from the same place! Why did God pick me to rise and my brother to fall? How am I supposed to enjoy myself, progress further from where I came, and leave my sibling behind to suffer? Was I blessed or cursed? It made absolutely no sense. He was older. He was more intelligent. He was a man. I remember something I read once in a book entitled *God's Little Answer Book*: "To trust in God means to move ahead with your heart when your head says it can't be done." Was that it? As a woman had I been able to trust more? To feel more of God? To quiet dominant thoughts and follow the dominant feelings? *It did not happen because you were a woman; it happened because you chose to allow it to happen. You are living the results of your choices.*

I was almost there. I had ten minutes to figure this out and fix my mascara. Mentally I made a column A and column B. In column A I listed the *truth* as I knew it.

My brother is a child of God.

My brother is endowed with all of the attributes of the Divine Mind of God.

God loves my brother and wants the best for him. God will give my brother anything he asks of Him.

God has always been with and will always be with my brother.

God will forgive my brother for all of his misdeeds.

God has sent my brother to earth to fulfill a divine mission that only he can fulfill.

My brother is alive through the grace of God.

God knows exactly what my brother needs, and is willing to give it to him at any time. Everything takes time.

What looks to me like suffering and struggle is the way my brother has chosen to learn his lessons in life.

God knows my brother better than I do, because my brother was created in the image and likeness of God.

I love my brother, but I cannot help him.

In column B, I mentally listed what was appearing before my face. More important, I listed my judgments and perceptions of the situation that were based on my own fears.

I think my brother uses drugs and alcohol as a way to escape his pain and fear.

My brother could die, and I would feel guilty about that.

I think my brother wants other people to feel sorry for him, and that makes me very angry.

My brother is wasting his life.

I want my brother to want for himself what I want for him because I think that will make him feel better. I know it would make me feel better.

I really don't know what plans God has for my brother.

When I see my brother I feel powerless.

I feel ashamed of my brother.

When my brother asks me for help, I get angry because I think he should be helping himself.

When I was where my brother is, I did not feel the way I feel now.

I am mad at myself because I seem unable to convince my brother that he can do better.

I really don't know what better is for him.

I really do want God to help my brother.

Oh my God! I wasn't crying for him at all! I was crying for myself. For my fear and anger! For my shame and guilt! Now that I've had this brilliant revelation on I-95, what am I supposed to do?! Love thy brother as you love yourself. Honor him by honoring his choices.

But he's killing himself!

The Father knows what he needs even before he asks!

But he's not even asking!

Praise the soil that the Spirit can grow in!

Praise my brother for wasting his life?

Praise the truth you know about him! Honor the truth you know about God!

But I'm really worried that something bad is going to happen to him.

Most of what you worry about never happens, and that which happens may come so unexpectedly you would not have worried about it anyway!

Don't I have a responsibility to help him?

Your responsibility to God and yourself is to honor him!

How do you honor someone who does such horrible things?

How do you honor the truth in column A!

So praise him for being a child of God who doesn't work, feels sorry for himself, uses drugs, and calls me to borrow money he never pays back? Praise him for dishonoring my mother and father? Praise him for not staying with his wife and raising their son? Praise him for waiting until he was was forty-three years old to get involved in criminal activity? Praise him for that? Honor that?

No, for that you must forgive yourself. That is not who he is. That is what you judge!

How can I praise him when I am so mad at him and afraid for him?

Praise him and see the good in him no matter what your eyes behold. See him as a spirit, not as a body. Praise him silently in your heart for being a child of God. Praise him openly because you love him. When he comes to you for help, help him in ways that bring you joy. When you cannot help him, tell the truth. Do not say you do not have when you do. That does not honor what God has given you. Do not say you cannot do, say you will not do. Honor yourself for the right to choose; in this way you honor him for the choices he makes. Only through the truth can the light and power of God remove darkness. Only when you honor your brother not as your brother but as a perfect creation of God can you honor the God within yourself.

DAY 17

Honor Others
with . . . BOUNDARIES

Working Definition:

The principle we are working with today is BOUNDARIES. They are mental, emotional, or physical constructs that define or limit the area in which one is willing to be present. The space or area in which one works, lives, desires to be.

Commentary on Boundaries

She was drunk, calling me, to borrow money. Again. I knew she wasn't working. I knew she had no place else to turn. I also knew that this could not go on forever. She could not stay drunk and dysfunctional forever, and I could not support a grown woman forever. She was, after all, just a friend. She was not a child or a family member. If that were the case, there may be some more responsibility on my part. Perhaps I could justify doing it then. But not now. Not under these circumstances. People have to learn to take care of themselves. They have to learn that they are responsible for their lives. If your life is not working, whose responsibility is it? What are we supposed to do when those around us cannot seem to get it together? How much is too much? How long is too long to give and care and support somebody else? Just thinking about it made me mad. The funny thing is, I was mad at myself for overstepping my boundaries and getting myself involved in someone else's life.

Ken Kizer, my rebirthing coach, told me, "When you don't have boundaries in your life, people will inject themselves into places in your life where you do not want them, and where they have no business being. Boundaries are like drawing a line in the sand and saying, 'Beyond here I will not go and you cannot come.' The key is to be very clear and very committed to what you are willing to do if the line is crossed." On the day he said that to me, I had come to the stark realization that my life had been like a big picnic ground, with everyone and everything all mixed together. Strangers were in my kitchen and my bedroom. Family members were rummaging through my very personal things. Business, social, personal relations were all entwined. Everybody knew everybody else, and everybody had something to say about everything. People were running amok in my life, and there seemed to be nothing I could say or do about it. There were no boundaries.

As I reflected on my personal situation, I could see it was a reflection of how I fit into the lives of others. I knew very personal details about the people who worked for me and with me. I knew far too much about people I associated with on a business or professional level. It wasn't just that I knew so much about so many people, I was actually involved in the intimate workings of their lives. When I wasn't giving advice, I was lending money. When I wasn't lending money, I was helping somebody out of or into a situation that had absolutely nothing to do with me or my life. Yes, you are expected to help people when you are able. Yes, you should share resources, exchange information, support those who need support. But when do you let go and allow people to figure it out for themselves? If you keep doing for people what they must learn to do for themselves, they will never learn to do it. This does not honor people. It does not honor you.

I had always been a caretaker. As a child, I took care of my aunt when she was sick from hypertension or depressed over her wayward husband. As a teenager, I took care of my stepmother when she was emotionally distraught over the lack of attention paid her by my father. As an adult, I took care of three children, a chemically addicted brother, a philandering husband, and a host of girlfriends who had the same or similar problems. Taking care of someone meant fixing whatever was wrong. If I could not find a way to fix it, I considered it my job to find someone else to fix it. If both of those efforts failed, it then became my job to defend or protect the aggrieved party. As a result, I was always involved in a dramatic production that had few if any positive effects on my own life. I used taking care of people as a clever disguise for not setting boundaries.

My caretaking efforts were not without a goal. As long as I was taking care of you, I was in control. Secretly, I was a control freak. I needed to know what was going to happen, when it was going to happen, how it was going to happen, and the role I would play in the happening. By taking care of people, I was in control of what they did to me, how they did it, when they did it, and if they did anything at all. I called the shots, which meant I could not be hurt. I could be used and manipulated, but that's different. When you are taking care of people, you are afforded the opportunity of seeing people at their worst, which usually meant they were in worse shape than you. I had a covert investment in seeing other people stay there. As caretaker, I got the chance to see people when they were weak, which meant I was not so weak. It's strange how being around weak people makes you feel stronger, even when you do not believe you are strong. Taking care of and being in control of the lives of other people takes time, energy, and attention away from the only thing you really have to deal with in life, yourself. However, in order to take care of yourself, you must have boundaries.

The call from a distressed girlfriend put me on notice that I needed to draw the line in the sand, again. I was running away from myself, again. I was fighting for control, again. I was supporting people in being weaker than me, again. My life was not going well at that moment, and I had been spending too much time fixing problems that were not my own, and becoming too deeply involved in lives that were not my own. If I set myself up to be a crutch, I would deny people the opportunity to learn what they needed to learn in order to stand on their own. Like me, my friend needed boundaries. She needed to know how much to drink, how much to spend, and when to stop before she got herself into trouble. If I continued to rescue her from her lack of boundaries she would never figure out how to make her life work. A lack of boundaries will not only make your life uncomfortable, it helps you help other people in making their lives uncomfortable. You cannot honor others when you support them in self-destruction.

If I lent her the money again, she would not pay it back again, which means I would be very upset with her, again. Where there are no boundaries the same bad decision has an opportunity to be repeated. I had too much to do. I did not need to be upset with myself or anyone else. If I did not make a statement about how her drinking was affecting our relationship this time, she would think that what she was doing was okay next time. Most important of all, I realized, this had nothing to do with an inebriated woman, crying about being put out of her townhouse. This was about my need to honor her choices and honor myself. I did not feel good about giving her the money, and if she were sober, she would probably not feel so great about asking me for it. We needed boundaries in our lives and in our friendship. It was on me to draw the line in the sand. "I do not feel good about you when you drink to the point that you are at right now. When you are like this I would appreciate not hearing from you. I also don't feel good about the coincidence of your being drunk and needing to borrow money for some essential part of your life. So let us establish that I am your friend. I am here for you if and when you need me. However, let that need not be tied to you taking care of your basics. Rent is a basic. Food is a basic. Getting to work on time is a basic. If you want to go shopping or on vacation, call me. I'll go with you, or I'll lend you the money to go alone. You take care of your basics, and I, your friend, will support you in getting the frills."

Commentary Journal

After reading today's commentary, I realize

The key phrase(s) I want to remember and work with today are

Morning BOUNDARIES Affirmation

In this place I am peace.
In this place I am light.
In this place I am joy.
In this place I am love.
In this place I am a divine idea in the mind of God, sharing the peace,
*   light, joy, and love of God.*
In this place I give.
In this place I share.
In this place I serve.
In this place I give, I share, I serve to the glory and goodness of God.
In this place I am a vessel.
A vessel of peace, light, joy, and love, giving and sharing the divine ideas
*   of God.*
My task is easy. My burden is light.
When it is not, I am not in my place.
And So It Is!

Let Me Remember . . .

BOUNDARIES allow me to take care of myself.

BOUNDARIES enable others to take care of themselves.

BOUNDARIES create the freedom of choice.

To give, share, or support need not mean taking care of.

I can say no and still give love and support.

BOUNDARIES keep me in my divine, right space.

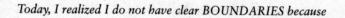

Evening BOUNDARIES Journal

Today, I realized I do not have clear BOUNDARIES because

Today, I was tempted to cross my BOUNDARIES when

Today, I realized it is necessary to have BOUNDARIES because

DAY
18

Honor Others
with . . . COMPASSION

Working Definition:

The principle we are working with today is COMPASSION. It is the ability to be one with others and sacrifice your needs for their needs without feeling depleted. Giving of self with the realization that you are in effect giving to self.

Commentary on COMPASSION

I wish I had a nickel for every time I have been told, "You simply cannot be too nice. People will take complete advantage of you and leave you hanging out to dry." One way to not be *too nice* is to be a little nice. Unfortunately, this rarely works. You can never seem to do enough when you are being just a little nice. On the other end of the scale is not being nice at all. This never works. When you are not nice to people it probably means you are angry. If you're angry, you spend a great deal of time justifying to yourself and others why you should not be, don't have to be, and are not nice. This will remind you of how and why you got angry in the first place. If you're not angry and are only having a momentary spell of insanity that makes you not act nice, you are probably riddled with guilt. Guilt never feels good. The way to avoid guilt and be nice without being too nice is to practice compassion.

Only when you have a healthy, honorable, affirming relationship with yourself can you have the same with others. This relationship is the foundation of your ability to demonstrate and practice compassion. Only when you have truly mastered yourself and are able to stand in your sense of personal power can you be compassionate. If this is not the truth of your being, your attempts to be compassionate will mean being too nice and you will become a doormat. You will believe that you are being used. You will feel put upon and eventually become resentful of all that you have done or are doing for others. It is only from a sense of true and authentic personal power that you can give, support, share, and assist without feeling that you are losing anything. When you are a powerful master of yourself you know that what you give is of the universal divine energy flowing through you. It is not yours. It belongs to life. When a powerful person gives life, s/he knows they cannot be depleted. Instead, they know they are being strengthened. You must be strong in order to be compassionate.

A compassionate person is not one who does for others what they must do for themselves in order to grow. A compassionate person is not one who jumps in and takes over or one who gives to the point of exhaustion or depletion. A truly compassionate person is one who can feel what you feel because they are one with you in mind, body, and spirit, not out of obligation or a false sense of responsibility. A compassionate person is one who understands what you are going through and, rather than joining with you in your suffering and fear, sees for you the lesson, the blessing, and the victory at the end. A compassionate person does not join in the victim mentality of blaming others; instead they will stand strong with you, supporting you through the acceptance of the situation. The compassionate person knows with you, for you, and when necessary in spite of you, that all things work together for your good. It takes vision to be compassionate.

What most of us call compassionate is a quest for power and control. Often those who consider themselves compassionate are those who try to be nice to others and, in doing so, end up feeling used and manipulated. Many of us believe that compassion is to see what someone needs, and to give it to them in order to make them and yourself feel better. It is hard to watch someone suffer. It's even harder when you are not suffering or struggling. When you see it, you feel bad for the other person and jump in to save them. Well, maybe they don't need saving. Maybe what they need is support in making a decision, or information that will help them reframe their situation so that they are empowered to handle it for themselves. We call it being nice, doing for others, helping someone less fortunate than ourselves. That is not compassion! That is martyrdom, because chances are if the situation does not turn out the way you think it should, you will be highly pissed. You will be mad at the person you helped and probably mad at yourself for wasting your time, your resources, and your energy. In order to be compassionate, you must know that the universe is an endless reservoir of resources.

Compassionate people do not help, they support, because they know that to support you means they will also help you heal and grow. Compassionate people ask you what you need and then respond to your request, not to what they think you should have. Compassionate people do not take your power; they help you find it by standing squarely in their own sense of power. There is not lack of love, peace, prosperity, or any good thing in this life. Compassionate people know this, and they want to support you in understanding the same principle. A compassionate person can walk the floor with you, they can give of their resources, they can pull you up when you ask them to. A compassionate person can do all of that without, in any way, feeling you owe them or that there is a predetermined result being sought. They want the best for you, not because they think they know what is best, but because your best is their best. You see, a compassionate person is in it with you for the long haul, with no expectations other than they are able to do what needs to be done.

In Native American tradition, compassionate people are those who embody snake medicine. Most of us are afraid of snakes, and it is no coincidence that many of us are also afraid of our power and of powerful people. We don't realize that the snake represents our power and ability to heal. A compassionate person supports others in the ability to heal themselves. To shed and still be whole. To be raw and vulnerable, yet continue the journey. Snake medicine is the knowledge that those things which are considered poison can be ingested, integrated, and transformed through the proper state of mind. A compassionate person is able to connect with your perceived suffering or pain and transmute that energy through the presence of their power. It is the power of thought, ambition, resolution, wisdom, and understanding that will always result in wholeness. A compassionate person wants you, as a universal being, to realize your wholeness. Your wholeness has nothing to do with being nice, and a compassionate person recognizes that your journey to wholeness may not look nice. Compassionate people have the ability to nurture, comfort, and provide nourishment to others at various stages. They heal without making themselves sick.

When you can set aside your needs and desires, becoming completely willing to give of yourself to fulfill the needs of another, you have discovered your sense of power, and that enables you to be truly compassionate. When you can feel another's pain, sense their fear, know what they are going through without considering them to be a victim or feeling your own sense of victimization, you are ready to demonstrate compassion. When you understand that what you do for another or give to another will in no way have an adverse affect on you, you have reached the realm of compassion. If you have the overwhelming need to jump in and save somebody for fear that if you don't they will pull you down, or if you cannot watch other people suffer because you are afraid if you don't help, the same thing might happen to you, you have not yet reached the state of personal mastery that enables you to be compassionate. If you are acting purely from the need to be nice, you are going to end up feeling used. Used people become victims who haven't got a clue about what compassion really means. Compassion is the way we honor ourselves and others by demonstrating what we have mastered. Few of us have mastered what it really means to be nice.

After reading today's commentary, I realize

The key phrase(s) I want to remember and work with today are

Morning COMPASSION Affirmation

I am one with all things.
I am one with all life.
I am one with all people.
I am one with the Divine.
In my oneness I am eternal and unlimited.
In my oneness I am able to give of myself to myself.
In my oneness I give what I am.
In my oneness I give freely, willingly, compassionately with love.
As I give to myself, I am strengthened.
As I give of myself, I am empowered.
As I give my all, the presence of eternal, unlimited divinity becomes the reality of my existence.
For this I am so grateful.
And So It Is!

Let Me Remember . . .

I am powerful enough to give what I have without losing anything.

I am one with everything and everyone.

Support + Comfort + Nourishment = COMPASSION

In my COMPASSION for you I am strengthening myself.

Everyone has the power to heal themselves.

Today, I found it was difficult to be COMPASSIONATE when

Today, I was able to demonstrate COMPASSION when

I now realize that my ability to be COMPASSIONATE is hindered by

DAY
19

Honor Others
with . . . CLOSURE

Working Definition:

The principle we are working with today is CLOSURE. It is a state of being complete through mental and emotional detachment. An act or actions that bring to a close the nature and status of a situation or relationship.

Commentary on Closure

He was dead. My father had died without ever having told me that he loved me. I was thirty years old, but it still hurt. I knew I was hurting because I was looking at my dead father without shedding a tear, but remembering that he had never told me, "I love you." Everyone was looking at me. I felt like I needed to be doing something besides remembering this unpleasant aspect of our relationship, but the truth was that most of our relationship had been unpleasant. I was remembering that too, right then, at the side of his casket. It felt very awkward and very painful. I wanted to touch him, but I couldn't. I wanted to say something to him, even knowing that he would not hear me. I needed to speak to him. I decided I wouldn't do anything at all except sit back down.

I spent the next several weeks trying to figure out why I could not cry for my father. Surely I would miss him as much as I would not miss the hostility that always seemed to exist between us. Because he had died peacefully, in his sleep, I knew he had not suffered. But he had suffered. He had suffered through a life of unfulfillment and mediocrity. He suffered through the embarrassment of never being able to provide for his family. Yes, he had suffered in life and was now at peace. Unfortunately, his being in a state of eternal peace had left a gaping hole in my heart. There had been so much I needed and wanted from my father that he was never able to give. I had long ago accepted this as a fact of my life. Yet, for some reason, now that he was dead all of the questions that had gone unanswered were racing through my mind. Was he proud of me? What was the real reason he did not attend my college graduation? Why had he left my mother? Most of all, did he love me?

When I explained to a friend how I felt, she told me that I needed closure. When you do not have the opportunity to express what you are feeling at the close of a relationship, the relationship is incomplete. It does not matter that the other party is no longer living; without closure in any relationship the people involved feel incomplete. Death, like separation, divorce, or the abrupt termination of any kind of relationship, evokes a tremendous amount of emotion that must be released. The release results in closure. When you do not release, you wonder, you hurt, the why's go unanswered and eventually create anger and fear. More important, my friend said, when there is no closure, you miss the lessons and the blessings. You are never really sure why this person was in your life, what you shared to your benefit, what you learned about yourself, and why you are better off, better equipped to move on to new and more productive relationships. When there is no closure you hurt. "How?" I asked, "can you come to closure if the other person is no longer living?" Write a letter. The issue is not that the other person read the letter; the issue is for you to have the opportunity to express what you are feeling.

Dear Daddy:

I know you are dead and that you will never read this letter, but it is my attempt to set us both free from the pain of our past relationship. I guess I should first thank you for being my father. If it is true that we choose our parents and that they consent to bring us forth into life, I do owe you my gratitude. I am glad to be alive, although I am not very happy about the way I have lived under your care. I don't want to point fingers or anything, but you did a pretty shitty job of caring and providing for me. I am sure you knew from your own personal experience that your mother was unnecessarily abusive, and still you left me in her care. Why did you do that? What was so important that you could not take care of me? You knew that she beat me! You knew that she screamed and yelled and called me names. She told me that you were running around in the street with women, and that you didn't care about me. And you never told me any different. You stopped by, patted me on the head, gave me a few coins, and went off on your merry way knowing that Grandma was torturing me. Why did you do that? Why? WHY? WHY?

Was I such a bad kid? Was I that ugly and fat? Were you ashamed of me or what? Is that why you never came to school for me? Is that why you never checked my homework or read me a story? Is that why you never came to my dance recitals? What did I ever do to you that you should treat me with such disregard? I was just a little kid. I didn't want to be ugly. You made me ugly! They were, after all, your genes! Do you have any idea how horrible it feels to be a little kid and have a father who acts like he hates you? I know you didn't really hate me, but you sure acted like it. I also realize that your mother, being as unaffectionate as she is, probably never taught you how to be affectionate. It was your responsibility to learn! I was your daughter! I needed you to kiss me, hug me, hold me, and treat me like I was special! Was I ever special to you, Daddy? Did you ever say to people, I have a little girl and she is very special? I sure hope you did, even though I never heard you say it.

I must also tell you that on my bad days, I hold you totally and completely responsible for my brother's destruction. I try to tell myself that he is responsible for his own life. I know that he has the same ability that I have to pull himself together and make something of his life, but I also know that people are different. He and I are not the same. Somehow I was able to move beyond the abuse, neglect, and dysfunction of our lives. My brother, your son, has not been that fortunate. He suffers every day. He is in so much pain, anger, and confusion that he sees no reason for living. Did you know that your son was an alcoholic? Did you know that he has been chemically addicted since he was nineteen? Well, of course you knew! The question is what did you do? What did you say? Did you know that he was angry at you for all the things you did not do for us? He believed that gambling, women, and money were more important to you than he was. He needed a father to show him the way, but you were never home! You were always too busy! But you weren't too busy to criticize him or complain about what he hadn't done, were you? Why did you tell him you would kick his ass? How could you say that to a fifteen-year-old boy that you hadn't seen in two weeks? Who the hell did you think you were to say that to him? That is why he left home, you know! He has been a total wreck ever since then! I have always hated you for what you did to him. He is my only brother. He was there for me when you weren't. And as a result of your lack of care, lack of attention, lack of interest, he can't be there for himself. I absolutely, unequivocally, with no sense of shame, hate you for the pain you caused my brother!

Did you love my mother? If you did, why did you bury her in an unmarked grave in the pauper's cemetery? Why didn't you borrow some money from your gambling buddies and bury my mother like a decent human being? Did you know that it took me two years to find where she was buried? She was buried in a grave with five other people! Five strangers who did not know that she loved you and bore your two children. What kind of man would do something like that to the woman he loved? Did you love her? If you did, why didn't you marry her? Why did you marry someone else while you were living with my mother? And why didn't you tell me any of this? Why did I have to find out the most intimate details of my life's beginnings from other people? Why did you lie to me? You were really a piece of work! I have tried to figure all of this out, and none of it makes any sense to me. Now you're dead, and I'm left here to sort through the mess.

I have tried to forgive you. There are times when I do pretty well. There are times when this madness makes absolute sense. You did the best you could with what you had. I know you did not have an easy life. I know you tried your best to make things right, but when you saw they were not going right, what did you do? You ran. You hid or at least that is what it looked like to me. You did not tell the truth. You did not ask for forgiveness. You never admitted you were wrong or apologized. Well, you know what, I forgive you anyway, on my good days. On my good days, I realize that you have taught me a great deal. You have taught me what not to do. You have taught me how not to be. You have taught me the importance of being there for my children. You have taught me the importance of telling the truth and letting people know what is going on. In addition, you gave me the most precious gift of my life. You gave me my stepmother, my best friend, my angel. Without her, I don't think I would have made it this far. She was to me all that you were not.

On my bad days I hurt, and I hate you. You want to know something else: Hating you makes me feel worse. It's hard to hate your father. It makes you crazy, and I have been crazy for far too long. I want to be at peace now, just like you. So I am writing to let you know that I will not have any more bad days. I will have only those days when I can have com-

passion for you and forgive you for lying, for leaving, for cheating on my mother, for abandoning me and my brother, and for in every other way not being the kind of father I wanted and needed you to be.

As of this very moment, I choose to remember only the good things I knew about you. That you were handsome. That you gave me my first car. That you bought me a washing machine for my wedding present and that, without any doubt, you loved your grandchildren. I will remember how you cooked for them. I will remember how you let my son sit on your lap and steer the car when he was only two years old. I will hold the vision of you coming to my front door to pick them up on Saturday mornings, and how you walked away with them hanging on your legs. You were an excellent babysitter, and they really loved you. I know they will miss you. Perhaps my children were still young and innocent enough to see the good in you. If I hold the memories of you and them in my mind, perhaps one day I too will see your good. I want that more than anything else. If I can remember the love you had for them, perhaps I will see that you really did love me in the only way you knew how. I know I loved you, and I guess I was just like you, because I never knew how to say that to you. Maybe now you will know it. I sure hope so.

When I put the pen down, I cried for my father.

Commentary Journal

After reading today's commentary, I realize

The key phrase(s) I want to remember and work with today are

Morning CLOSURE Affirmation

Today, I surrender, I release, I detach from every person, every circumstance, every condition, and every situation that no longer serves a divine purpose in my life.

Today, I realize that all things have a season, and that all seasons must come to an end.

Today, I realize that all things fulfill a divine purpose to support my growth and evolution as a unique and noble expression of life.

Today, I realize that there is no end. There is only now, and this now begins a divinely new season and purpose in my life.

Today, I choose a new beginning over the pain-filled memories of the past.

Today, I choose a new season, filled with purposeful thoughts and activities.

Today, I choose to close the door to yesterday and open my mind, my heart, and my spirit to the blessings of this moment.

In this moment, I am filled with light. I am filled with joy! I am filled with love that brings divine understanding!

For this I am so grateful!

And So It Is!

Let Me Remember . . .

People come into your life for a reason, a season, or a lifetime.

CLOSURE begins by telling the truth about what I feel.

I am entitled to honor what I feel.

When one door closes, another door opens.

Whatever you repress will become stress.

Evening CLOSURE Journal

I realize it is difficult to bring CLOSURE to a situation when

Today, I was able to bring CLOSURE to

I realize I must continue working to bring CLOSURE to my thoughts and feelings about

DAY
20

Honor Others
with . . . NONJUDGMENT

Working Definition:

The principle we are working with today is NONJUDGMENT. It is a state of mental and emotional openness and receptivity to new experiences and new interpretations of past experiences. Observation of people and/or participation in events without the imposing of personal will, perceptions, or criticisms.

Commentary on NONJUDGMENT

Every parent wants their child or children to be the very best they can be. Along with this very natural, very normal desire comes the parent's perspective of exactly how good the child can be and how they should go about demonstrating that goodness. Parents have rules, parameters, and guideposts that measure how well the child is doing. Although they don't like to admit it, I think most parents also have a time line. They want it done this way, by this time. They say it is for the child's benefit. Parents know, you know, what happens to idle hands and minds. Not only did they read it in the Bible, they have also witnessed what has happened to their own peers and the offspring of their peers who were not fully committed to the pursuit of becoming good. When the offspring fail to demonstrate satisfactory progress toward the goal of goodness, parents naturally assume the kid is off smoking weed or gambling over in the devil's workshop.

I know a lot about this. You see, I am the parent of three offspring. One was born good and never strayed off the path. Another had some vague idea that good existed, and tried desperately to figure out where it lived. Another, I judged, could not identify good if it jumped up and bit her on the butt. None of my offspring are dead, so all of this was subject to change. Before the change could take place I went into fear. In the midst of my fear, I subjected them all to the natural, normal parental judgments, comparisons, criticisms, and hysteria that threatened to destroy our relationship. I judged them to be irresponsible, unfocused, uncommitted, and downright lazy. I learned from a very dear friend that what I was looking at had absolutely nothing to do with my children. I viewed them by the judgments I had made about myself.

I came from a dysfunctional, impoverished background. I got pregnant at sixteen. I dropped out of school. I married young. I had a bad marriage. I struggled to raise my three children alone, hoping, praying, and doing everything in my power to ensure that my children did not make the same mistakes that I did. I wanted more for them. Admittedly, I had no idea what the more was or what it would take to get it, but I thought I knew very well the things that would push them along the same path I had traveled. I was always on the lookout for those things. The things I had done. The things I had said. The behaviors I had exhibited. Whenever I saw signs of me in my children, I became angry. Angry at them for what I thought was risking their lives, and angry at myself for what I had done to stray away from being good. Once the anger subsided, I became afraid. Afraid that they were not going to make it to goodness, and afraid that I would fail them the way I judged that my parents had failed me. I could see the cycle of dysfunction repeating itself from my parents to me, from me to my children. It made me crazy!

It's so good to have a sane friend to talk to when you are crazy. I had one. My friend made one statement. It was a simple statement that made no sense and so much sense at the same time. He gave me some insight that helped me release my children, myself, and every other person and condition in my life from the death grip of judgment. The statement:

"There is no right, no wrong, there just is what is!"

Are you telling me that it's not wrong to kill, lie, and steal?

People who commit those acts do so in fear, shame, or guilt. Is it wrong to be afraid or shamed, or to feel guilty?

It made sense, but it didn't feel right, I mean good. I had to pursue this line of thought a bit further. If there is no right or wrong, that means anybody can do anything because they are afraid, ashamed, or guilty.

People do anything and everything anyway. The fact that we judge it wrong or right does not stop people from doing anything in this life. When we judge what they have done, we are actually informing them of the conditions we place on loving them. When they do what we think is right, we love them. If we judge them wrong, we become angry and ignite the fear that we will take our love away. A person without love is a frightened person. A frightened person is capable of doing some pretty unloving things.

Get a grip! Thousands of people were enslaved because somebody felt unloved? Hitler killed millions because he felt unloved?

I had it backward.

That with which we are unfamiliar, we fear. Those things we don't understand we fear. People are enslaved by or because of fear. When we feel powerless we seek power. When we have no control we seek to control. People are killed when powerlessness seeks to control.

That's crazy!

Crazy is a judgment.

People killing or enslaving other people because they are afraid or because they feel powerless or want control is not crazy?

Who's to say? People do what they do based on who they are, what they believe, and the information they have at the time that supports their feelings and beliefs. Slavery is wrong today. Four hundred years ago it seemed like a viable economic venture. Hitler is considered a monster today. In his day, however, thousands supported or ignored him. Saying it was right or wrong does not change the fact that it was. When you think of something as wrong, you are actually saying there is something wrong with you.

ME?? I don't think there is anything wrong with me!

Of course, you do. That's why you judge your children.

I'm not judging my children. I simply want them to do the right . . . thing. I mean I want them to make out better than I have.

What's wrong with the way you made out?

I made it so hard on myself and those around me.

You did what you knew how to do based on what you knew and believed to be right at that time. How can you prevent your children from doing the same thing if that is what they choose to do?

By teaching them how to do things the right way. By giving them better skills, better tools than I had. You've made me afraid to use the word "right."

When you are afraid, you see and hear things that have nothing to do with what is. Your children are going to do whatever they are going to do, no matter what you think, say, do, or fear.

I know. Good kids come from bad homes. Bad kids come from good homes. There must be some magic formula to ensure the success of our children.

There is. Give them your best. Share with them what you know, and let them make their own choices based on what you have shared. When they falter or fall, be there for them without anger or fear. Take the conditions off your love. Stop looking for your mistakes in their actions. When it is all said and done, the best thing you can do for your children is to stop believing that there is anything wrong with the way you turned out, or the way you turned up.

I hate it when you're right.

I'm never right. I just share what I know because I am.

You must mean, "You is!"

After reading today's commentary, I realize

The key phrase(s) I want to remember and work with today are

Morning
NONJUDGMENT Affirmation

I am, because God is in control.
All is, because God is in control.
Every person and every living thing has at its life's center God's perfect
  control.
I will not judge by appearances.
I will not fear when things do not go my way.
No matter what it may look like, I must remember, God is always in
  complete and perfect control.
For this I am so grateful.
And So It Is!

Let Me Remember . . .

There is no right or wrong, there is only is.

People do what they do based on their feelings and beliefs,
which are not right or wrong.

I do not understand what I am looking at, so I must not JUDGE what I see.

I always JUDGE others by the JUDGMENTS I have made of myself.

JUDGMENT closes the mind and heart to new levels of understanding.

No matter what it looks like, God is in control.

Today, I realized I am quick to JUDGE myself when

Today, I found myself JUDGING others when

I realize it is easy to suspend JUDGMENT when

DAY 21

Honor Others with . . . FORGIVENESS

Working Definition:

The principle we are working with today is FORGIVENESS. It is release. Letting go. The process of removing errors from the mind in pursuit of harmony. The release of what is false for what is true. Giving up of a thought or emotion in order to facilitate change of the thought or emotion.

Commentary on FORGIVENESS

"How long are you going to stay mad and hurt?" I didn't know, but I knew I was not ready to not be mad yet. What she had done to me was unforgivable! Besides that, somewhere in the back of my mind I actually believed that the longer I stayed mad, the more she would suffer. After a while, what she had done was no longer the issue. The issue was her suffering. She had to suffer! And I wanted everyone to know that she was suffering because of what she had done to me! I wanted to read about her suffering in the newspaper! Then and only then would I even consider not being mad at her anymore. She must have known I was mad at her, because one day she quietly died in her sleep. I wanted to say, "Good for her!" But I was too mad. Many, many years after her death I was mad, I was miserable. I was still hurt, and she was still dead. Now, what kind of sense did that make?

Most people believe that when you forgive someone, you are doing something for them. The truth is, when you forgive, you are doing it for yourself. As it relates to forgiveness, you must give up what you do not want in order to make room for what you do want. You must give up pain, anger, resentment, and fear in order to experience goodness, joy, peace, and love. For some reason, we believe that if we forgive someone they might get to the good stuff before we do. Offering another the forgiveness they need strengthens the spiritual nature in you. It is this nature and your consciousness of this nature that reaps you the benefits of life. When you withhold forgiveness or love from anyone, for any reason, it diminishes your awareness of the abundance of good in life. You are stuck in so much old stuff, new stuff has no way of getting to you. In essence, the good that you withhold from others will be withheld from you.

As long as you hold on to the belief that anyone on earth can do anything to you, you will be unable to forgive. People cannot change who you are and what you were born to be. They can create obstacles in your path. They can do things that make you believe you are other than what you are, but people cannot change, alter, or in any way hinder the truth of your being. The truth is you are divine. The truth is that the divine source of life made you perfect and complete, and nothing anyone does can change that. The truth is we all forget that we are divine and act out of our human fears, beliefs, and perceptions. In doing so, we offend one another's sensibilities, we ignore one another's boundaries, we lash out, strike out, and in other uncompassionate ways dump our pain on one another. It does not change who we are. It makes us believe we are less than we are. This makes us mad, and in holding on to our *madness,* we refuse to forgive.

There is no one who does not make mistakes. Mistakes are a way of human life. We mistake what we see for the truth. We do not realize that there is always more to life than we can see and that the truth is not always visible to the naked eye. We mistake what we know for all there is. What we do not realize is, we don't always know the whole story. At any given time in your life, there are characters, plots, and story lines that have not yet been presented. When you do not know the whole story, almost any conclusion you draw will be a mistaken conclusion. We mistake our experiences, particularly bad experiences, to be indications of who we are and what we deserve. Even when we know we deserve better, we mistake our experiences for the obstacles that can keep us from experiencing more. Sometimes, we make the mistake of thinking that other people have the power to control or alter our destiny. It is our beliefs, mistaken and otherwise, that ultimately determine what we will do or be in life, not another person.

If we did not make mistakes we would not learn what works and what does not work. Each time we make a mistake we are provided with an opportunity to be corrected. The divine spirit of life is self-correcting. It will show us our mistakes in the form of the pain and suffering that we endure. It will show us our mistakes through mental unrest and emotional dissatisfaction. Unfortunately, when we encounter the results of our mistaken beliefs, choices, and perceptions, we blame other people. We hold others accountable for what we think, feel, or believe. We believe our experiences make us who we are in life, and then we blame the players in our experiences. The biggest mistake we all make is believing that other people can hurt us. When we believe they have done so, we are unwilling to forgive them.

My aunt refused to acknowledge that my uncle, her husband, had raped me. She acted as if it did not matter. Translation: I did not matter, and what he had done to me did not matter. I concluded that she didn't care about me, that he was wicked, that I was dirty, and that life in general sucked! I held onto the memory of that experience, and my translations, conclusions, and the anger for a very long time. When a counselor asked me how long was I going to stay mad, it was sixteen years, three children, one bad marriage, and several heartbreaking relationships later. "What do you want her to do?" she asked. I wanted her to acknowledge me. I wanted her to acknowledge that what he had done was wrong. "And how would that make you feel?" "Better!" I said. Since my aunt was dead, she suggested that I needed to find another way to feel better. She suggested that I try forgiving my aunt for not acknowledging me, and for making the mistake of believing that if she had acknowledged what her husband had done it would have meant the end of her marriage. I told her she was out of her mind!

When being hurt and angry and believing you are less than you are does not get you what you want, it is time to forgive. When you cannot move beyond the memories of what someone else has done to you and those memories keep you hurt, angry, or in any way limited in life, it is time to forgive. When the only thing you remember about someone is what they did to you and not the fact that they are a human being prone to make mistakes, it is time to forgive. When you believe you know the whole story of why someone did what they did and believe that if they had done anything else, you would be different, it is time to forgive. If you don't like yourself, it is time to forgive. If there is anyone, anywhere on the planet you can honestly say that you do not love, it is time to forgive. If you are overweight, underweight, out of cash, in a bad relationship, working in an unfulfilling career, have corns on your little toes, have a cold or a toothache, there is somebody, somewhere you need to forgive. Start with yourself. Forgive yourself for believing that anyone who occupies the flesh form as a human being could in any way alter the truth of your being. Once you've done that it will be easy to forgive anyone for anything, particularly if you are holding them hostage for making human errors.

After reading today's commentary, I realize

The key phrase(s) I want to remember and work with today are

Morning FORGIVENESS Affirmation

I am now ready and willing to receive the perfecting presence of Spirit in my life.

I now open my mind and heart to the divine understanding of Spirit.

I now FORGIVE myself for every thought, word, and deed I have embraced or undertaken that has kept me from the realization of the truth about myself, and the perfect unfolding of the divine plan for my life.

I am now ready and willing to receive the perfecting presence of Spirit in my life.

I now open my mind and heart to the divine understanding of Spirit.

I now FORGIVE everyone for every thought, word, and deed they have embraced or undertaken that has kept them from the realization of the truth about themselves and me, and the perfect unfolding of the divine plan for our lives.

I FORGIVE all! I release all! I am now free from all except the perfect and Divine plan and purpose for my life!

For this, I am so grateful!

And So It Is!

Let Me Remember . . .

God has always FORGIVEN me.

I can FORGIVE myself.

To FORGIVE is to be free.

Being angry or hurt will not get me what I want.

What I withhold from another will be withheld from me.

Today, I realize I have been unwilling or unable to FORGIVE because

I realize that I would be willing to FORGIVE_____if

I now realize the need that being unwilling to FORGIVE has

DAY 22

Honor Others with . . . SERVICE

Working Definition:

The principle we are working with today is SERVICE. It is the ability to give of self (for example, time, knowledge, resources) without an attachment to the expectation of reward or recognition. Working with a consciousness of love (unselfish giving).

Commentary on SERVICE

We are rarely taught to serve in life. We are taught to work. Work, we are taught, is the act of doing what needs to be done in order to acquire the things that we need. Work, we believe, is necessary to our ability to survive in life. Work, as it is done in this society, is the ultimate measure of our value in life. The more we earn as a result of the work we do, the higher the value we place on ourselves. We work not for the pleasure of it; we work for the reward and recognition. Although there are many forms of work in which we provide a service to others and to the world, our attention is generally focused on what we get and the outcome of what we do. This is not service.

Service is the act of doing what you love for the sake of loving it. This is the highest work you can do in the world. Service is the divine multiplier. When you perform an act of genuine service, giving of your time, energy, and resources as an act of love, the universe will multiply what you do and reward you with greater results than expected. Love sparks the fires of passion. Passion leads to spontaneity and creativity. Spontaneous creativity is a supreme act of trust. When you trust yourself and the universe enough to give yourself over to the passion of what you love, you are serving humanity and the Divine.

Have you ever wondered why so many people hate their jobs? Perhaps you are one of the people in this category. If so, then you already know that most of us hate what we do for work, hate the environment that we do it in, hate the people we do it with, or are sorely disappointed by the rewards we get. Most of us think that if the rewards were greater, the conditions were better, the people were nicer, we would feel a lot better at our work. This is what we think, but for the most part it is not true. When you subdue your passion to focus on reward and outcome, there is no expression of love. The foundation of human nature is that we need love. We crave love. We grow in a loving environment. It's not the money that is missing from the workplace, it is the love. It is the service.

I graduated from law school believing that I could best serve the world and humanity as a legal servant. The problem was, I was not proud or fond of the premise of the legal system. As it is written, everyone is equal, everyone has the same rights, rights must be protected, and the system should not discriminate on the basis of race, gender, age, or any of the inherent characteristics of human beings. As much as we want to believe that it does, the legal system simply does not function this way, and I was often ashamed of the way the system works. I did not like being part of the system. I did not like the operation of the system. I did not like the people in the system. After a while, I did not like myself for being in the system. And I made pretty decent money, but it wasn't enough to bring me joy or peace. I was not serving. I was collecting a paycheck.

Dr. Susan Jeffers wrote a book entitled *Do What You Love, The Money Will Follow*, which teaches about the value of having passion for what you do. My own experiences have taught me that service, doing what you love, has rewards that money cannot buy. It has also become very clear to me that when you give yourself over to acts of love, passionately spending your time giving of yourself, you are never at a loss or lack for the things that you need. Believe it or not, we need much more in life than money. We need a sense of purpose. Purpose keeps you from being burnt out. Service gives you purpose. We need a personal mission that will help us focus our time and energy. When you are on a mission, you have passion, there is an internal fire that keeps you alive. Service keeps you alive and well. We need a sense of connection that makes us feel worthy. When you feel worthy you know you are valuable, and you intuitively want to take care of yourself. Service gives you a reason to take care of yourself.

There is a big difference between service and working for the sake of getting something. When you serve, you are not tied to the outcome. You are not invested in what people do as a result of what you do, or what people think about what you are doing. You give what you have because it makes *you* feel good. You give what you have because you know that the unique way in which you do what you do will make someone else feel good. In situations when your service is not rewarded by monetary or public recognition, you are not depleted or defeated. You are encouraged to take your service to a higher level. You are inspired to pour more love into your work. Jesus Christ mastered the art of service. He gave of Himself for the evolution of others. He had no vested interest in the outcome. As a matter of fact, He rarely, if ever, got paid. Instead, His joy came from serving others for a higher purpose. His purpose was His own spiritual growth and evolution.

For many of us, the kind of service Christ offered the world is a bit farfetched and distasteful. Who wants to be stoned, chased, or hung in the name of love? Certainly not me! I do, however, want to live a life where the contributions I make, the work that I do, the purpose I am serving, will have a lasting effect on humanity. I do want to be remembered. I do want to be cherished. I do want to know love. If you think about it, you probably want the same things. These are the rewards of service. You may never know in this lifetime how your work and contributions made in love affect people. However, when you give a service, this is not your concern. You do what you do because you love to do it. Whatever you love will touch somebody. Even one person calling your name, singing your praises, honoring what you do is more than many people ever get in this life.

Service, as a spiritual principle, does not imply or import poverty. Most of us think that if you serve, giving of yourself without focusing on the money, you will be poor. How, we think, can I work and not be concerned about money or rewards? We are taught that if you work hard and give your best, you should be richly rewarded. There is a problem with this line of thinking. How much money can you make working in the mail room? You can work your little tush off, sorting those letters and licking those stamps, and chances are you will never make enough to be what is considered wealthy in monetary value. However, if you think of your work as service, if you do it with love, if you value yourself and your position, the rewards will come in many others ways. There is also a big chance that the passion you exude will attract someone's attention and you will be moved, advanced, promoted to a position in which you can provide a greater service. Unfortunately, most of us would not consider employment in the mail room an honorable position. Chances are we would be so concerned about how much money we are not making that we would hate our work, the environment, and the people. Where there is hate, there cannot be love. Where there is no love, there is no service.

Do what you love! Do it with passion! Do it with the understanding that if you are never rewarded with money or recognized by the public, you are making a valuable contribution to yourself. Shift your focus from money to love. When you have love, you want to give of yourself. When you give of yourself for the sake of love, the impersonal, immutable, perfect laws of the universe demand that you must be rewarded tenfold. Stop worrying about survival! You have survived! You will survive! Understand that when you serve, when you give to the universal multiplier, you will be rewarded. You will be taken care of. Do not measure your value and worth by external standards. Do not compare yourself or what you do in love to what anyone else is doing. If you wait for someone to tell you that you are great and to reward you for that greatness, and it never happens, you may convince yourself that you are living a worthless existence. You are divine. There's a great deal of worth in your divinity. You must love your divine self enough to know that everything you do must be an act of love. Giving of your divine self in the name of love is the highest honor you can pay to those around you.

After reading today's commentary, I realize

The key phrase(s) I want to remember and work with today are

Morning SERVICE Affirmation

Today, I recognize that I am a child of the Divine; sustained by divine love, guided by divine light, protected by divine mercy, alive through divine grace.

Today, I am thankful for this gift of life through which I am able to SERVE.

Today, I ask the Divine to use me.

Use my mind. Use my eyes. Use my ears. Use my hands. Use my feet.

Use my being and this gift of life to SERVE those in need.

Use me as an instrument of peace. Use me as a tool of strength. Use me as a vessel of patience and healing and love that I may SERVE those in need.

Let all that I am today be in SERVICE to Your will.

Let all that I do today be in SERVICE of Your love.

Let all that I give today be in SERVICE and alignment with your perfect plan for humanity.

Today, I am in Your SERVICE.

For this I am so grateful!

And So It Is!

Let Me Remember . . .

To SERVE is an act of love.

My SERVICE is a divine gift to the world.

When I do what I love, I am richly rewarded.

Service and poverty do not coexist.

Passion + Focus + Purpose = SERVICE

When I give SERVICE, survival is guaranteed.

Evening SERVICE Journal

Today, I realize the difference between the work I do and the SERVICE I can give is

The one thing I could do for the rest of my life, whether I got paid or not, is

The things that keep me working instead of SERVING are

Phase Four

*"God can heal a broken heart,
but he has to have all the pieces."*

FROM GOD'S LITTLE DEVOTIONAL BOOK

Honor What You Feel

There is nothing more frustrating than someone telling you that you *should not* feel something when you are feeling it. Don't they realize it's too late now! You are already in the midst of feeling it! Whatever the emotion you are experiencing at the time, someone *shoulding* on you usually does not help you get out of it. As a matter of fact, just hearing what you *should not* do will either push you deeper into the feeling or make you feel guilty or ashamed. Guilt implies that there is something *wrong* with what you are doing. Shame implies that there is something *wrong* with you because of what you are doing. Since we now understand that there is no *right* or *wrong*, we must also understand that we have a right to feel whatever we feel.

Unpleasant or negative emotions are merely expressions. They let us know that there is something in ourselves or our lives that is not being expressed at the highest possible level. Since most of us have been shamed or made to feel guilty about what we feel when we feel it, we have become afraid of our feelings. For myself, some of the most damaging experiences of my childhood stem from being told I was wrong or being punished for expressing what I was feeling. "Shut up! Don't cry! It doesn't hurt!" Such comments told me that what I was feeling was not real or important. "Don't touch that!" said that natural inquisitiveness was not a good thing. "Don't say that! It's not nice!" translated into the suppression of emotions and self-doubt. There are many admonishments we hear as children that eventually result in not being able to trust what we feel, and not knowing what to do about it when we feel it.

Emotions, or feelings, as we call them, are the energies that move us in response to our thoughts and experiences. All emotions are neutral. They have no meaning other than the meanings we assign to them. An emotion is like a burst of energy that quickly circulates through the mind and body, indicating that there is an imbalance of energy that needs to be brought into balance. Balance as used here means neutrality or being void of meaning. When a thought or experience impacts the conscious mind, the energy begins to move throughout the mind and body, attaching itself to every like energy that already exists. This means that if a thought or experience evokes anger in you today, it will find and attach itself to every thought or experience that ever caused you to feel the same way. Whether your first experience was at age three or five or sixteen does not matter. The energy of the experience remains in your subconscious mind. Fear, shame, guilt, love, joy, peace—all operate in the same way. Consequently the things that evoke emotion from you today are expressions of the same things that evoked these emotions the first time you experienced them. This theory leads many psychologists to say that you are never frightened, angry, guilty, or ashamed for the reason you think you are. The reason presenting itself before you today is the most recent experience, the *last straw,* so to speak.

What goes on in our lives and the experiences that we have at any given moment is rarely the issue. We are responding to meanings and judgments we attach to the experiences, and it is our judgments that create imbalances in our mental and emotional energy. When you add to this the influences of the world that tell us that what we are feeling is wrong, the result is inner conflict. Conflict makes us beat up on ourselves. Like attracts like. Conflict in our mind and emotional nature attracts conflict from the world around us. The normal human response to conflict is blame. We look for and point to those people and experiences that have given rise to the imbalance of energy, the emotion we are experiencing. It is then that we find ourselves embroiled in fear, anger, more conflict, and the inability to express what we feel. In the worst-case scenario, we express what we feel in inappropriate ways such as violently striking out, screaming, or cursing. Even these expressions are not bad or wrong. They are inappropriate and socially unacceptable.

You have a right to your thoughts and feelings. You also have a right to act in response to what you think and what you feel. Your actions are a reflection of who you are and what you believe to be true about yourself. Remember, *Thought + Word + Action = Results.* There are predetermined boundaries that we are expected to adhere to, and it is our attempt to stay within these boundaries that creates conflict in our emotional being. Boundaries are for the protection of others. They do not determine the validity of what you are experiencing. Your feelings are always valid. The challenge we all face is to understand what we are feeling and to de-charge or neutralize it, thereby making it possible to express the feeling at the highest level possible for the good of everyone involved. When you are angry, you are angry. When you are afraid, you are afraid. What we must each learn to do is to get beneath the feeling and root out the cause in order to bring our mental, emotional, and spiritual energies back into balance. This requires a great deal of work. It also requires having the courage to examine and explore our inner conflict. It demands patience with self and others. Most important, it requires the willingness to go back in order to go forward.

I am not trying to suggest here that if your mate, child, or supervisor does or says something that makes you angry, you should stop, rewind your mental tapes, identify when and how you first experienced anger, and try to express that feeling at this time. What I am asking you to do is to elevate what you feel to the highest possible expression. Do not deny what you feel. Just keep in the back of your mind that it will pass. I am asking you to feel what you are feeling, when you feel it, and to admit to yourself and, if appropriate, to the other person that you are feeling it. You are always in control. The moment you experience a burst of emotionally charged energy, suspend all judgment of yourself for feeling whatever it is and ride it out.

Trust yourself enough to know that you can feel anything and recover from it. Know that because you are feeling something does not mean you must act on it at the moment you are feeling it. Stay with it long enough to de-charge it. Breathe deeply. If you can, write down what you are thinking and feeling, and then destroy the piece of paper with all the fervor you can muster. Above all else, for the first thirty to sixty seconds of the experience, please practice KYBYS. This ancient principle, pronounced "kib-biss," will ensure that you find the appropriate expression for any emotional imbalance. KYBYS means "Keep Your Big Yap Shut!" Pull yourself together and allow your brain to refocus! Ask yourself, "Self, what is the real issue here?" In sixty seconds or less you will know exactly what to do. That's just how divine and powerful you are. Later, when you can get off by yourself, you can practice some of the things outlined in this journal. You will not fall apart. You can move through any situation with your dignity and self-respect intact. Just remember to practice KYBYS!

Emotional Neutralization Process

There are no quick fixes for emotional imbalances that require healing. Healing is an ongoing process. However, there will be moments when we must do something to provide ourselves with temporary relief and release from negative experiences and emotions. This chart is offered not as a quick fix, but as a process by which you can find temporary relief from the experience of a negative emotion. Most things offered here can be done in sixty seconds or less. It means you must be willing to tell the truth and not pass judgment on yourself or anyone else because of the temporary experience of a negative thought or feeling. It also means that the moment you get the opportunity, you must make the commitment to take this process to a deeper level and heal/neutralize your emotional being. By doing the following, you may find it easier to move through the experience without hurting yourself or anyone else.

When You Feel	You Can
Angry	Take several deep breaths.
	Give up the need to be right.
	Forgive yourself.
YOU MUST PRACTICE Forgiveness	Forgive the person who has evoked the anger.
	Put yourself in the other person's place and speak to them, saying what you would want to hear under these same circumstances.
	Tell the person how you feel and ask if you can continue the conversation later.
	Call on the Divine and ask that your mind, heart, and words be tempered with love.

When You Feel	You Can
Confused	Identify what you really want.
	Admit what you really want to yourself.
YOU MUST PRACTICE	Do not judge what you want.
Meditation	Let everyone involved know what you really want.
	Identify what you perceive to be the issues facing you.
	Make a plan to handle one issue at a time.
	Write the plan down.
	Follow it.
Disappointed	Examine your intent.
	Admit your true intent to yourself.
YOU MUST PRACTICE	Admit to yourself whether or not you told
Truth	everyone involved your true intent.
	Forgive yourself for not being honest.
	Make a new plan that will get you what you really want.
Doubtful	Breathe.
	Suspend all judgments.
YOU MUST PRACTICE	Pray for guidance.
Patience	Detach from the outcome.
Frightened/Fearful	Breathe deeply.
	Examine your expectations, that is, what you are expecting as an outcome.
YOU MUST PRACTICE	Examine your intent, that is, why are you
Trust	doing whatever you are doing?
	Detach from the outcome.
	Call on the Divine for strength, support, and guidance.
	Remind yourself of everything you can be grateful about.

When You Feel	You Can
Guilty	Admit what you have done to yourself.
	Admit what you have done to another person.
YOU MUST PRACTICE	Examine your motives and the information
Acceptance	that was available to you at the time of the act. Be honest.
	Forgive yourself.
	Ask someone to forgive you for what you have done.
	Explore the ways you can compensate someone for what you have done.
	Perform at least one act of compensation.
	Remain conscious of what you are doing at all times.
Lonely	Hug yourself.
	Go to a quiet, open field or park and lie on the ground.
	Remember those who love you and the times you felt loved.
YOU MUST PRACTICE	Pray and ask the Divine to fill your heart
Service	with love.
	Examine your intent, that is, why you did what you did.
Unappreciated	Examine your expectations of others.
YOU MUST PRACTICE	Forgive yourself for judging others.
Nonjudgment	Do something nice for a stranger.
	Write yourself a love letter.

DAY
23

When You Feel
...ANGRY

Working Definition:

The emotion we will work through today is ANGER. It is the response to built-up frustration. A rebellion against authority. The experience of having one's sense of personal power denied or infringed upon.

Commentary on ANGER

How do you handle anger? Do you stuff it? Do you blast somebody? Do you lie to yourself and others, saying you are not angry when you are? Do you believe that a person of your intellectual, spiritual, or social standing is *not supposed* to get angry? How did you see anger acted out as a child? How did you feel when someone was angry with you? What were you willing to do to make things okay again if someone was angry with you? (Don't you hate it when people fire a series of questions at you before your brain can compute them?) I believe that anger is one of the most powerful emotions a human being can experience. Perhaps it is because the impetus for anger is passion. Passion is the driving force of life. Unfortunately, when we do not know how to process and express our anger, we also seem to have difficulty expressing our passion.

"You are never angry for the reason you think you are" is one of the basic premises presented in *The Course in Miracles,* a psychological construct designed to create a shift in perception. *The Course,* published by The Foundation for Inner Peace, teaches that anger is the ego's response to the belief that it is being attacked. The ego believes it can be attacked because it believes that we are all separate beings. However, since we are all one in the mind of God, it is impossible to be attacked because God cannot attack Itself. It takes a deep desire as well as a great deal of study and time to integrate the principles of The Course into your consciousness. In the meantime, most of us try to figure out what to do about being angry when we are angry. And we all feel justified about feeling that way when we feel it.

My son and I went to retrieve some artwork that had been framed. We parked in the tiny parking lot several yards away from the shop. When the art was ready, my son pulled the car up to the door of the shop. Although he was blocking several cars parked in the lot he popped the trunk, walked ten or twelve feet to the door, and picked up the artwork I had placed there. Because there were ten large pieces, we would have to make a few trips, but we were never out of sight of the car. The loading should not have taken more than three minutes. As we were moving back and forth, a wonderful gentlemen cleverly disguised as a frantically angry and bitter lunatic told my son to move his car. My son said, "Oh, excuse me. I've only got to get a few more things." The gentleman said, "Move the car NOW!" My wonderful son said, "OKAY! Just a minute!" If the man had gotten in his car, put on his seat belt, turned the engine on, and shifted the gears, we would have been gone. That would have been too simple. Instead, he told my son, "I SAID NOW!"

A twenty-six-year-old who has been out of prison for three weeks can only take so much verbal abuse in a parking lot. He inquisitively asked the man, "Who are you talking to like that?" "I said, move this car!" Slowing his pace to a crawl, my son said, "Well, now you will wait!" The man reached into his pocket. I thought he was going for a gun. He pulled out a quarter, ran three feet to a public telephone, picked up the receiver, looked at my son, slammed the receiver back into the cradle, turned to my son, and screamed, "Where's your Christmas spirit?" It was then I knew that the lights were on and nobody was home! Whereas my son had been carrying two wrapped pieces of art at a time, he now carried one while he whistled and looked up at the sky. Before either of them could open their mouths again, I spoke to the man. "Please forgive us. It will only be a minute more." Leaving the telephone and walking back to his car, the man responded to me, "Whose car is this?" My son was still creeping and whistling. "Mine," I said. "Well, get it the hell out of my way!" It is amazing how anger can turn a very simple situation into a major dramatic production. My son shoved the picture he was carrying into my chest, knocking me back against the car. Turning and lunging toward the man in one movement, he screamed at the top of his lungs, "Don't you talk to my mother like that!" Now I knew we were really headed for trouble. I was screaming my son's name, telling him to get in the car. The man, who was now trying to find his keys as my son got closer to him, was screaming repeatedly, "Move the car or I'll smash it! Move the car or I'll smash it!" He was driving a Lexus. I was driving a fully insured Honda. My son was screaming at the man, "That's my mother! That's my mother!" Finally I screamed, "Damon, he didn't do anything to me. The poor man needs healing! Now get in the car!" Time stopped. My son stopped. My heart stopped. The man jumped in his car and revved it up. I got behind the wheel and pulled out of the parking lot. Just as I expected, the entire scenario took about three minutes. The angry exchange made it seem like an hour.

The Course teaches, "The worse people act, the greater is their need for healing." When we experience anger, there is something inside calling out for healing. Do you believe that you are a separate being struggling for survival in life? Are you rebelling against authority? Do you believe that your personal space has been invaded? Do you feel powerless? Unacknowledged? Unloved? Who are you really angry with? Yourself? A parent? Your first true love who left you for someone else? Why are you angry? What has this person actually done? Why do you think they did it to you? What kind of assumptions are you making about this person? What judgments have you made about them? About yourself? All of these questions and more are underneath the temporary experience of anger in which you currently find yourself.

My son was enraged. I told him to take a deep breath and another. It helped to bring his mind into focus. "What happened to you?" I asked.

"He's a pig?"

"That's not the question. What happened *to you?*"

"He had no business talking to you like that!"

"He didn't do anything to me. He has a right to say whatever he wants to. We were out of place. We were blocking him."

"He could have waited. He had no business talking to my mother like that!"

"Maybe that's how his mother talked to him. Maybe he was in a hurry. Maybe his wife left him this morning, and he was on his way to find her. Maybe his son is a crackhead. That is not the issue. The issue is we were blocking him in, and he has a right to feel anyway he chooses to feel about it. Our job was to move the car as quickly as possible."

"He's just like those prison guards. They used to talk to me like that, and I didn't like it then. I don't like it now. In there I had to take it. Out here, I don't! He's a pig and I treated him like a pig."

"He's your brother, and he deserves to be loved for being the pig that he is."

"Ma, you are taking this spiritual love stuff a little bit too far!"

"Perhaps I am, but what is the alternative when you are in a parking lot screaming at a wonderful child of God who is cleverly disguised as a pig?"

My son took another long, deep breath and said, "I can't figure out how to make sense out of nonsense."

"Stop trying, Damon, just keep breathing. Sooner or later it will become clear."

After reading today's commentary, I realize

The key phrase(s) I want to remember and work with today are

Morning ANGER Affirmation

This is the day of divine expression.
I will seek nothing but joy in this day, knowing that all things are working
    together to bring me healing, so that I may be a greater expression of
    Divine Love.
For this I am so grateful!
And So It Is!

Let Me Remember . . .

I have a right to feel what I feel.

What I am feeling is a temporary experience that cannot harm me.

All things work to bring me healing.

People act out of the need for healing.

I can choose what I feel about any experience.

Forgiveness will provide relief and release.

Love will heal anything that is not an expression of love.

Evening ANGER Journal

The experiences I had today that evoked ANGER were

I responded by

I forgive myself and am willing to be healed of feeling

D A Y
24

When You Feel . . . Confused

Working Definition:

The emotion we are working through today is CONFUSION. It is the experience that results when one does not admit what they want or need in any given situation. Knowing what to do, and not demonstrating the courage required to get it done. A response to fear.

Commentary on CONFUSION

Chaos and confusion are not the same things. Chaos is the energy we create when we have a need to be needed, when we want to make ourselves feel important, when we are trying to convince ourselves we are not important, and when we need something to do. Chaos looks confusing, but it is not confusion. Chaos is a cleverly disguised way of saying, "I know what to do and you don't!" Or, "You know what to do, so please rescue me!" Or, "Get out of the way! I'm in control here!" Or, "There is something else I need to be doing, but I can't do it now because I'm busy creating chaos!" Confusion, on the other hand, is a mental and emotional response to the failure to admit what we really want, because we are afraid we will not get it.

Confusion is an experience of having the brain shut down. There is a barrage of information coming at you, and you can't figure out what is real from what is unreal. The natural response is a perceived experience of not knowing what to do. Well, that's impossible! You always know what to do because you have a divine connection to the One Mind that knows everything. Confusion is also the mental and emotional outgrowth of knowing exactly what to do, and having this knowledge clouded by the belief that you are not good or smart enough to do it. This is augmented by the fear that if you do it, you might not do it right, or that if you do it the way it needs to be done, somebody will get mad at you. The natural response to this self-defeating mental chatter is for the intellectual mind to shut down. The result is what we call confusion.

There was a time in my life when I was very confused about why I couldn't sustain a lasting, meaningful relationship. It seemed as if I would never have a fulfilling or lasting relationship with a man, and that friends would always betray me. I told myself that it wasn't my fault, and that I had done the best I could in every situation. I finally retreated into the self-debasing judgment that there was something wrong with me. As confused as I was and damaged as I believed I was, I kept dragging myself in and out of relationships and friendships. The confusion eventually spread to my career. I could never seem to figure out what my supervisor wanted. I never seemed to do anything right. From there, the confusion spread to my finances. I could not figure out why I never had enough money, why I kept bouncing checks. Where was the money going? I was putting it in the bank.

Confession is another important step toward the elimination of confusion. I confess, I was not willing to ask the men in my life for what I wanted because I was afraid they would leave me. I confess, I was not willing to tell my friends when they were overstepping their boundaries because I thought they would be mad at me. I confess, I was not handling my finances with attention and care because I thought there was never enough to do what I wanted to do. I confess, I believed I was ugly, too fat, not smart, unworthy, unvaluable, and a disappointment to my mother and God. The result of not confessing these things to myself about myself and taking healing steps toward correction was confusion. The final straw came when I lost my car! No, it was not stolen. I lost it in the parking lot. I parked it right under the big letter C. When I returned from my shopping expedition, it was not there. It took me forty-five minutes to find my car right where I had parked it—under the big letter F. F stands for fog. My brain was fogged by my unwillingness to ask for what I wanted.

Until you are ready to admit to yourself exactly what it is that you want, you will experience confusion. Until you are willing to ask for exactly what you want in life, from any situation, or in your relationships with other people, you will experience confusion. The confusion will not subside until you honestly believe that you deserve what you want; that you are entitled to the experience of what you want; and that, if it is for your highest good, you will eventually have exactly what you want. In order to move out of confusion, you must be willing to be still long enough to get in touch with what you really want. This can be a pretty frightening experience, particularly when there is negative self-talk and negative chatter going on in the mind. You can alleviate this kind of disruption with self-affirming thoughts and actions. Once this is done, and you identify what you want, you must be willing to mentally and emotionally ride out the experience of admitting what you want. Stop worrying about how and when it will happen. Realize that you can have in life only what you are meant to have. Everything you receive is for your growth and healing.

Once you have admitted what you want, consciously take steps toward the realization of that experience. Do and say the things that are a reflection of your desire. Do not settle for something you know is a reasonable facsimile of what you want. Hold out for the real thing to show up. Ride out your dream. You will know it when it shows up because it will meet every aspect of what you have said you want to experience. In the meantime, keep affirming yourself. Be willing to admit when you make a mistake. Ask for help or support when you need it. As you move toward your goal and gather new information, realize it is never too late to change your mind. As soon as you realize the need to make another choice, admit it to yourself, and then do it.

After reading today's commentary, I realize

The key phrase(s) I want to remember and work with today are

Morning CONFUSION Affirmation

The divine presence of life, love, joy, peace, and goodness knows what I want before I ask for it.

This Presence is unlimited and abundant.

This Presence supports my right to have unlimited good and abundance.

Today, I will ask for what I want, knowing that the divine presence within me will lead me to that which is for my higher and greater good.

For this I am so grateful!

And So It Is!

Let Me Remember . . .

The Divine knows my needs and desires before I ask for them to be met.

All the Divine has is mine by divine birthright.

I am entitled to the best life has to offer.

I can ask for what I want and expect to receive all that is for my own good.

In the midst of CONFUSION I will be still and tell the truth.

I confess that I have believed I am

I confess that I have believed life is

I confess that I am ready to have

D A Y
2 5

When You
Feel . . . DISAPPOINTED

Working Definition:

The emotion we are working through today is DISAPPOINTMENT. It is failure to realize a desired or expected outcome. Thoughts grounded in the fear of losing control.

Commentary on DISAPPOINTMENT

I really wanted my children to go to college. My son went into the Navy. My eldest daughter went to college for two semesters, lost thirty-five pounds, and begged to come home. My youngest daughter barely got out of high school. Needless to say, I was disappointed. I had so many dreams for my children. I wanted one doctor, one lawyer, and one college professor. I would have settled for an architect or an engineer, but I really had my heart set on a college professor, a Dr. Vanzant. Instead I got a disc jockey, a vice president in my company, and a nurse's aide. I guess I could have done worse, but I couldn't help feeling disappointed.

My first husband also disappointed me. I took our vows very seriously. Honor, cherish, sickness until death. Instead I got adultery, violence, sued for divorce. Disappointment is not only about what happens to us, it is also about what we do or do not do for ourselves. I have at times been very disappointed in myself. The things I have or have not done. The choices I have made. The chaos and conflict I have created in my life has at times been very disappointing. It was through self-examination that I found the root cause of disappointment: not stating your true intentions very clearly at the outset of any endeavor. When you fail to do that, and when you fail to let everyone involved know exactly what it is you want, chances are you will be disappointed.

I really didn't care whether or not my children went to college. I really wanted them to make me look good. I did not want to feel like a failure since I had them when I was very young. I did not want to stay married forever. I was just happy somebody wanted me and my young son. I have never been incapable of accomplishing anything I was equipped to accomplish or set out to accomplish with a good intent. Most of my life, however, has been spent doing what I thought other people wanted me to do. When it didn't work out the way they wanted it to, they were disappointed in me and I became disappointed in myself. Whatever you do without a clear and honest intent will leave you in some state of disappointment.

It is fantasy to believe that people can disappoint you. The only thing people can do is what they can do. They may say they can do something else. They may want to do something else, particularly if that something else will please someone they hold in high regard. We go merrily along with people, believing they will do what they say, even when their track record, demonstrated inability, or exhibited lack of interest tells us otherwise. In the end, we say they disappointed us. No. We are disappointed that we put our faith in this person despite our better judgment. People always show you who they are. It does not matter what they promise you; if you check the record of your relationship with most people, you have definite evidence of who the person is. You know whether or not they keep their word. You know whether or not they show up on time. You know if they will pay you back or not. We know because we always know, and still we act like we do not know when we retreat to the fallback position of being disappointed.

I have heard many people say that they were disappointed when they did not get the position, or the house or the money. I always ask why. There is a spiritual principle that says you can only have what is for you to have. Regardless of how much you want it or think you need something, if it is not in the divine plan for you to have it, you will not have it. There is nothing to be disappointed about. On the other hand, there are those situations when something is divinely ordained for us and it comes along, but we are not ready for it. In these situations, things will seem to slip right through our hands. The feeling is one of disappointment and devastation. The lesson is to get prepared. You cannot lose. Your blessings have your name on them. When you are ready, an even better opportunity will be presented to you. When it shows up, you will need to be ready. In the meantime, don't be disappointed.

Another sure road to disappointment is to do something you know is not quite right with the hope of getting something out of it. I think the term is ill-gotten gain. In most of these situations, you will be disappointed. The spiritual principle is that you cannot get something for nothing. You cannot gain something good if someone else will be harmed in the process. The laws of the universe will not permit it. You cannot buy a twenty-three-inch color television in the supermarket parking lot for $75. You cannot have a lasting, peaceful, and totally fulfilling relationship with a person who is married to someone else. We can twist and turn the circumstances, telling ourselves anything we need to hear to justify our actions, but our good can never grow from someone's harm. When we are not in alignment with the law, when we do not tell the absolute truth to ourselves and the other people involved, we will find ourselves in a sea of disappointment.

I have three wonderful children, whom, as they are adults, I call offspring. They are honest, dependable, loving people. I realize that the choices they have made in their lives they had a right to make. I understand that their failure or success will come in response to the standards they set for themselves. I recognize that they are still young and have plenty of time to make new choices and take their lives into new directions. I hope one of them turns toward medical or law school. I hope one of them will eventually have Dr. in front of their name. However, rather than wasting my time and energy being disappointed if they don't do it, I have done it for myself. I have a Dr. I have a law degree. I have been a visiting professor in several universities. You see, that is the key to never being disappointed: When you really want something, don't make anyone else responsible for you getting it.

Commentary Journal

After reading today's commentary, I realize

The key phrase(s) I want to remember and work with today are

Morning DISAPPOINTMENT Affirmation

*I now willingly release all negative beliefs about myself, my life and all
   other people.*
I now forgive myself for thinking I ever did anything wrong.
I am now filled with the love and the Power that I am.
For this I am so grateful!
And So It Is!

Let Me Remember . . .

Intent is always revealed in the outcome.

No one else is responsible for what I want.

My blessings have my name on them.

I can only have what is mine by Divine Right.

I cannot lose.

Lack of honesty always reaps a lack of satisfaction.

Evening DISAPPOINTMENT Journal

Today I experienced DISAPPOINTMENT when

I recognize that the way I deal with DISAPPOINTMENT is by

The thing about myself that I have found to be most DISAPPOINTING has been

When You Feel . . . DOUBT

Working Definition:

The emotion we are working through today is DOUBT. It is a state of conflict regarding the acceptance of truth. The onset of mental, emotional, and spiritual weakness. The absence of trust.

Commentary on DOUBT

It is a proven scientific fact that no two things can occupy the same space at the same time. This theory applies to the mind and heart of human beings. Where there is trust there can be no doubt. The moment doubt enters, trust has disappeared. You cannot believe and doubt. To believe is to know, understand, and accept the immutable truth. The truth does not change. The truth cannot be altered. Where there is total, unquestioning reliance on the truth, there can be no doubt. Doubt enters our consciousness and invades the mind when we forget the truth, and when we do not trust in the omnipresence of the divine law.

Doubt is bred in the mental state of attachment or emotional investment in the outcome. When we have a fixed idea of how things should be and how we want them to look, we become doubtful that we will get what we want. The doubt stems from our beliefs, many of which hinge on our thoughts and feelings of unworthiness. When we believe we are not worthy of having what we want, we doubt that we can or will receive it. Doubt is also the mental and emotional response to our need to be in control. To be in control we must know everything about everything. We fix our sights on a particular outcome and a method of achieving that outcome. When it appears that our plans are going awry, the natural response is fear, which is the primary ingredient of doubt. Control-based doubt is what we call worry. Worry is the direct descendant of the need to be in control.

What we must realize is that we cannot see everything. We do not know everything. More important, we must understand that it is impossible for us to control anything. The process of life is a spiritual one, governed by invisible, intangible spiritual laws and principles. When we are in alignment with those laws and principles, we experience the natural outcome of the laws in action. The laws bring into manifestation the will of God. This is a will for the good of everyone. When we understand and embrace this truth, there is never a reason to doubt. We know that no matter what it looks like, the final outcome will be something good.

We attract into our lives that which we focus upon with the strongest intent. Unfortunately, most of us do not monitor our thoughts, and therefore have no idea of what we are thinking about most of the time. Even on those occasions when we do focus, do plan, do concentrate on our intended desire, we evaluate our progress toward achievement by the appearance of physical evidence. We evaluate and judge what we see as the determining factor of our progress toward a desired end. When one predetermined element fails to appear as we have determined it should, we doubt ourselves and our progress. The moment a seed of doubt becomes imbedded in our thoughts, we can become so preoccupied with fixing what has apparently gone wrong that our thoughts shift from the desired outcome. We are now focused intently on ensuring that nothing goes wrong. Forestalling wrong, rather than desired intent, becomes the focus. That focus will ultimately grow into the very thing we fear, the failure to obtain the desired outcome.

Constant prayer and affirmation are the strongest defenses against doubt. Praying for guidance and believing that we have received it will bring our actions into alignment with Divine Will. Affirming the truth about ourselves and life will set into motion the spiritual principles of divine order and divine timing. We always get exactly what we need when we need it, even when we are not aware that we need it. Learning to live without having to evaluate every appearance, while remaining focused on our desire, knowing that it is an outcome of a good intent, leaves no room for doubt to grow in the conscious mind. Intent is the energy that supports expectation. Expectations always determine results. When we expect to be guided and protected and to receive the benefits of Divine Will, we can expect the results of all endeavors to be favorable.

Commentary Journal

After reading today's commentary, I realize

The key phrase(s) I want to remember and work with today are

Morning DOUBT Affirmation

Merciful, Divine, Blessed Spirit of life, Thank you for this day.
Thank you for this life.
Thank you for your divine presence in me and as me.
May you establish peace, plenty and joy in my world according to Your
*   perfect plan for my life.*
I trust you today to bring into my world all that is mine by divine right.
For this I am so grateful.
And So It Is!

Let Me Remember . . .

God is in control.

Where there is trust there is no DOUBT.

Truth is more powerful than DOUBT.

Where there is worry, there is a struggle for control.

What I focus upon with good intent must come into being.

The universal spirit of joy, whose desire it is for me
to have an abundance of everything good.

Evening DOUBT Journal

Today, I found myself worrying about

I struggle to be in control because

I realize I can trust the process of life because

DAY 27

When you feel . . . FEARFUL

Working Definition:

The emotion we are working through today is FEAR. It is the absence of trust. Ignorance of truth. Dread, dismay, disquiet. Fear is an acronym for False Expectations Appearing Real.

Commentary on Fear

I was forty-something. She was my friend. I was doing what I thought was necessary to maintain our friendship. For all intents and purposes, I was five years old again. I was afraid that if I did not do what she wanted me to do, she would not be my friend anymore. She had no malicious intent. She was in the midst of her own childhood fears. That is where we learn about fear. How to deal with it, camouflage it, function under the pressure of it, and run to get away from it. As my friend Rene Kizer would say, "I was alone in my head without adult supervision," trying to save something I thought was essential to my survival. In the process of being a friend, I created total chaos in my finances and in my family and intimate relationships. In the end, the friendship was drastically altered and the person was removed from my life.

Few of us truly understand the number of masks and disguises fear wears in our lives. I learned, the hard way, that what I called being a good friend was fear. Fear of losing control. I also learned that what I called procrastination was fear—fear of failure and success all boiled into one. After many toxic entanglements, I discovered that what I had so self-righteously called, "Look what they did to me!" was actually fear. Fear that I wasn't good enough. Fear that they would find out the truth about me. I had to get away. I had to sabotage the relationship before they discovered what I thought to be the truth about me. Following an IRS audit, I discovered that failure to keep accurate financial records was indeed fear. Fear that there was not enough. Fear wears so many clever disguises it is virtually impossible to always recognize it. What we can do, however, is embrace fear. Make it an ally instead of an enemy.

In her book *Building Your Dreams,* Mary Manin-Morrisey writes, "You cannot master a foe you don't recognize." She was writing about fear. I am sure I am not alone when I confess that there are many things in my life I have not done in response to the fear I have had about doing them. Many times, I did not know I was afraid. In those situations where I knew I was afraid, I was afraid to admit it. Instead, I devised all sorts of creative ways to get out of doing what I feared. The results: Fear mastered me. It dictated my movements and responses in any given situation. Fear has disguised itself as what I could not do, did not have, and did not have time to do, and as what others would not let me do. I have disguised fear as the need to be somewhere else, doing something else, not knowing how to do something, and not needing to do something. I set a table in my life for fear to become a gluttonous and insatiable master.

A few years ago, the city planted a row of young trees in my neighborhood. They were carefully planted and anchored with cords attached to metal poles in the earth. Each morning, as I took my walk, I would pass the young trees. On particularly windy days, I would watch the trees bend with the wind. Sometimes it would seem as if they were about to snap. They didn't. They flowed with the wind and stayed anchored. Fear is a common response to a strong wind in our lives. Something new, something old and reoccurring, something unknown coming upon us unexpectedly will evoke fear. At these times we must remember that we are anchored in the energy of the divine source of life. We must learn to bend and believe we will not break. We must hold on to what we know about our ability to weather the storm. This is how we can use faith to starve fear.

Mary Morrisey states, "The point is not to get rid of fear. Instead, we must embrace it as a companion." We must learn to recognize when we are in fear, admit when we are in fear and then dismantle the fear with the strongest tool in the human arsenal: faith. "Starve fear with faith!" is what she says. This means, when you acknowledge that you are afraid, you are reminding yourself to call forth your strength, your spiritual self. Rather than wasting time and energy running away from the things we fear, we can stand our ground, thereby developing the courage required to move beyond the fear. In order to do this, we must become still enough to tune into what we feel. We must learn to acknowledge and accept the signals and symptoms of fear when it approaches. Does your head spin? Does your heart race? Does your mouth become dry? Do your ears get hot? How does fear show up at the table in your life? Once you learn to recognize that fear is sitting around waiting for a meal, you can starve it with prayer or trust or by affirming the truth.

Today there are a vast number of spiritual teachers, spiritual books, and spiritual life practices promoting one consistent theory: "There are only two emotions: love and fear." Love is divine. Love is the activity of God, and the only energy in which God exists. Fear, on the other hand, is a tool of the ego, which is the foundation of the belief that we are separate from God, separate from each other, and generally inferior or inadequate. Think about it. When you are asked or expected to do something you do not believe you are worthy or equipped to do, is fear not the first emotion you experience? Fear of being abandoned. Fear of being ridiculed. Fear of having someone take their love away from you. Fear of being exposed as inadequate or unworthy. At the core of our innermost being, we do not want to feel this way, so we deny that we do. We lie to the master. "I'm not afraid, I'm busy." "I'm not afraid, I just don't want to marry you!" "I'm not afraid, I'm broke!" We fail to realize that the only way to pull the chair from beneath fear is to love it. In order to love fear, we must call the power and presence of God into our lives or the situation, allowing its presence to dismantle the fear.

The next time your stomach flips with fear, don't deny it by acting like you are just fine. Gently whisper, "I know you, fear, and I know exactly what you want. Unfortunately, today I am not in the mood to deal with you!" When your mouth gets dry, your knees get weak, or your ears get hot, don't call it menopause or something you ate for lunch. Embrace the fear that is now pounding its fork and knife on your table by saying, "Hi, fear! What took you so long to get here? Sorry, but I cannot feed you today!" The minute you realize you are in the grip of fear, don't struggle to get away. Relax! Tell the truth. "I'm in the grip of fear!" Remembering that truth will set you free. Freedom means choosing to invoke this truth:

"Wherever I am, that's where God is!" Take a few deep breaths. Affirm "Let there be light!" Fear hates the light of truth. The moment you affirm the truth, fear will scatter like the lower life forms that dig around in the garbage. If, however, you insist on telling yourself that you are not afraid when you know that you are, fear, the lowest form of life, will sink its teeth in you and never let go.

After reading today's commentary, I realize

The key phrase(s) I want to remember and work with today are

Morning FEAR Affirmation

I now consciously and willingly call forth the light of the Holy Spirit into every molecule, every atom, every cell, every tissue, every organ, every muscle and every system in my body, asking It to release every energy, every belief, every pattern, every thought, and every belief that is not in alignment with the love of God.

For this I am so grateful!

And So It Is!

Let Me Remember . . .

Wherever I am, God is.

Fear wears many faces.

If it is not love, it is fear.

Love will overshadow fear.

The light of truth will overshadow fear.

When I embrace fear, it becomes my ally.

False Expectations Appearing Real are not the truth.

Faith will starve fear.

Evening FEAR Journal

Today, I recognize that I was experiencing FEAR when

When I am FEARFUL my body responds by

When I realize I am in the grip of fear I am now willing to

DAY
28

When You Feel . . . Guilty

Working Definition:

The emotion we are working through today is GUILT. It is the judgment or belief that there is something wrong about what you have done. A learned behavior. An unmet need for approval.

Commentary on GUILT

This was by far the most difficult part of this book to write. The manuscript was late, which meant that I had failed to honor my agreement. I felt guilty about that. Each day I would promise myself to sit down at the computer and knock off another fifty or sixty pages. To my dismay, something more enticing would present itself, making it seemingly impossible to work on the book that day. What enticed me were things like shopping, eating, cleaning out the closet, or watching *Oprah*. No matter how hard I tried to resist them, these things always got the best of my attention while the book got very little. I felt guilt about that too. When my editor or agent called, or if either of them would cross my mind, guilt would grip me. I would freeze just long enough to beat myself up for not keeping my agreement, for not doing what I promised myself I would do, for not having more discipline, for being female in America, for using Hellman's instead of Miracle Whip. After a few moments of self-flagellation, I would be so depressed I needed chocolate to help me feel better. I'd eat the chocolate, knowing it would induce a psychological high that would put me to sleep rather than inspire me to write, which gave me something else to be guilty about.

There are two toxic emotions, guilt and shame. Shame implies that there is something wrong with me. Guilt implies that there is something wrong with what I have done. If the two were in a race and I had to place a bet on which would more quickly destroy my life, I would put all of my money on guilt. I seem to have been able to function within the confines of my perceived ugliness, inadequacy, limitation, and ignorance—I guess because I could show up anywhere dressed nice, smelling good, with my mouth shut and be able to overcome those parts of my humanness. However, when I had convinced myself that I had done the wrong thing, thereby imposing a sense of guilt upon myself, the web became far more complicated than my humanness could handle. Guilt kept me frozen in shame. It catapulted me into suspended animation. The more I fought to break free of its grasp, the tighter the grasp would become. People would call to ask me, "How's the book coming?" As I puttered around the kitchen searching for a new recipe, my children would admonish, "You better go write that book." When I announced, "I'm not coming to the office today," some wise person would always respond, "Good. You're going to stay home and write, right?" Knowing full well I was planning to pop some corn and watch *General Hospital,* sheepishly I would respond, "You know it." In all the hours between *Regis and Kathy Lee* to the evening news, I would shove popcorn in my mouth in an attempt to rid myself of the guilt of not writing.

How many times have you asked yourself, "What's wrong with me? Why do I keep doing the same thing over and over? Why can't I stop this or that?" Guilt and shame, walking hand in hand through the garden of your life, can create havoc! When you feel bad about yourself and/or what you are doing, it can be quite challenging to keep moving, or keep doing anything positive. It seems as if you are powerless to change. Powerless to stop. You want to, but you cannot. You become so preoccupied with trying to figure out why you did what you did that you keep doing it. The law: What you focus upon will grow! When you focus on what is not right, or on how what you did is not right, you stay in a state of "not rightness." It's called guilt. I have discovered that the only way to break free of the web of guilt is to confess what you have done, forgive yourself, and choose something else. Confess! Tell somebody that I made a mistake, told a lie, did not do what I said I would do for no reason other than the desire to watch *Oprah*? You must be out of your mind! I could never do that! The mere suggestion of it not only makes me feel more guilty, it pisses me off! Now I'm guilty and mad! This is called denial.

When we fall into denial about feeling guilty, the plot really thickens. In this state of mind, we must find reasons and excuses for the things we have done or not done. We blame. We become the victim of something or someone that kept us from doing or made us do what we have done or not done. Victims, like most guilty people, are powerless. Those who blame, like most guilty people, are helpless to choose or change. The plot of guilt has victims and villains wallowing in the mud of powerlessness and helplessness. How is a mere mortal supposed to stand up and move on in the face of this dramatic production? It's real simple! Confess, to yourself, what you have done, forgive yourself and choose something else. Does this mean I must tell other people, if other people have been harmed or dishonored by what you have done or not done? That means they will get mad at me. Ask them to forgive you too. The people you hurt don't forgive you? That's not your issue. But they won't like me anymore. That's not your issue. I need my mother's, father's, brother's, sister's, spouse's, friend's, children's love. You also need to love yourself enough to own what you have done. But it's hard. Only if you make it hard. Well, how do you make it easy? Just do it! Okay!

When I could have been writing this book, I chose to watch television or go shopping or give myself a pedicure or bake a cake or do the laundry or make love or play with my makeup. As a result of what I did, this manuscript was turned in two months late. My agent and editor were harassed by the copy editor and the sales force. The entire work schedule of many people I don't even know was thrown into chaos, and I spent several weeks in the grips of guilt and stress, wasting precious time I could have used to complete this project. I forgive myself for behaving in such a thoughtless and unloving manner. I ask everyone involved to forgive me also. As of this day, I choose to spend no less than four hours a day working on this project until it is complete. I make a covenant with myself and the Holy Spirit to honor this agreement. If at any time, for any reason, I am unable to keep this agreement, I will offer to myself and all others involved enough love to renegotiate the agreement. Now doesn't that feel better? It sure does!

Commentary Journal

After reading today's commentary, I realize

The key phrase(s) I want to remember and work with today are

Morning GUILT Affirmation

I am always free to choose.

My choices are always in alignment with the will of the Divine.

If for any reason my choices do not result in joy, peace, harmony, and balance, I am always free to choose again.

If my choices do not bring forth the best in myself and others, I am free to choose again.

A defective choice is not a reflection of the truth about me.

The truth is, as I see the manifestations of the choices I make, I am always free to choose again and again and again.

For this I am so grateful!

And So It Is!

Let Me Remember . . .

I am always free to choose.

I can forgive myself and ask for forgiveness.

I cannot lose true love.

Truth is empowering.

I can confess what I have done and renegotiate my agreement.

God loves me no matter what I do or do not do.

Today, I experienced GUILT when

I congratulate myself for moving beyond GUILT regarding

It was difficult to overcome this experience because

DAY 29

When You Feel . . . LONELY

Working Definition:

The emotion we are working through today is LONELINESS. It is an experience of isolation resulting from the belief in separation. The emotional response to being shut down.

COMMENTARY on LONELINESS

When we are lonely, we usually crave the companionship or love of another person. We experience intense anxiety where we believe that everything would be better and we would be better off if we had another person in our lives. We want to be loved by another person. In direct conflict to the urgency of the need to be loved is a subconscious shut-down to being loved. Somewhere in the back of the mind is a fear of love and/or a fear of what being in love will mean. We may have been hurt, abandoned, or rejected in the past, and while we can consciously convince ourselves that we are over it, the evidence of being lonely tells the true story.

I thought I had never been lonely. I have always been surrounded by people. I have always known that there was somebody somewhere who loved me. There have even been those rare occasions when I have been able to fully experience the warm presence of God's love. The times in my life when I was not involved in an intimate relationship were by choice. In response to those choices, I have missed people and yearned for their company, but I had no memory of ever being lonely. Then I discovered what loneliness means and realized I had been lonely most of my life.

Loneliness or the experience of being lonely, I have been told, is any emotion that is wrapped in anxiety or urgency. The anxiety creates a lustful craving that can never be satisfied. The urgency creates a fear that the very thing you are lusting for is in some way being denied or withheld from you. The key element of the fear and lust is that you are shut down to the very thing you want. You are either unwilling or unable to receive it because of a fear of what it might do to you.

Someone once asked me, "How much love can you stand?" I considered it a weird question until I thought about it. I thought about all the conditions I placed on being loved. I thought about how I wanted love to be demonstrated to me. I had to acknowledge that I had a belief that if someone really loved me, they would know all about me, and that, I thought, would not be a good thing. I also acknowledged that I kept most people I professed to love at an arm's distance, never allowing them to know too much or get too close, because I was afraid of being hurt. My mouth was saying I wanted to be loved, while my mind was thinking I was unworthy. I was sending out signals indicating that I wanted to be loved, but I would only let so much love in. My fear, which I am sure is the same fear for many of us, is that too much love would kill me. I would simply melt in its presence.

I remember when I first saw my son: five pounds and thirteen ounces of sheer beauty. He was absolutely flawless and beautiful. I knew he could not see me, as he was only two minutes old, but I could feel the trust and the love pouring off of him as I held him in my arms. He was my first child. He had no judgments of me. He wanted only one thing from me: to be loved. The experience took my breath away. I actually could not breathe. In the span of two minutes, I thought of all the reasons I was unworthy and undeserving of his love. I thought of all things about myself that needed fixing and changing. I thought of all the things I could not offer him. I was sixteen. I had a brand-new baby and no husband. I was a high school dropout, trying to breathe. It was more than I could stand, and in that moment, I think I shut down a piece of my heart. It stayed shut down for many, many years.

I have loved the same man for thirty years. The mere sight of him makes my knees buckle. He is the only person I know who has never made me feel anything but beautiful and wonderful. For thirty years, I could not have him. That made me want him even more. He was married. I was married. He lived in one place. I lived in another. I did not think there was an urgency to my wanting to share my life with him; however, there was a lusting after the way he made me feel. Our first attempt to be together was a sheer disaster. Neither of us were ready. Neither of us was open to the full expression of love. Neither of us could figure out how to accept the love we tried to give one another. It took him thirty years to tell me he loved me. It took me thirty years to be able to hear it. When he said it and I heard it, I stopped breathing and tried to get away from him as fast as I could.

To be lonely is to be shut down to the thing you want. You cannot have love if your heart is closed. You cannot have money if you are afraid of it. You cannot have freedom if you are unwilling to make choices. You cannot have peace if you think it means you must give up something essential to your survival. The absence of all of these divine potentials are at the root of being lonely. Most of the time, we are totally unaware that we are shut down. We are unaware that we are afraid. In response to being unaware, we seek and crave or lust after the very thing we believe we cannot have. This is the true meaning of being lonely. We are never lonely for a person or a thing. We are seeking an experience we believe we cannot have. When you find that you are experiencing loneliness, open your heart. Ask the spirit of the Divine to fill you with love. When you feel it, remember to breathe. It will not kill you. Allow love to fill your entire being. The moment you can do this, open your heart and yourself to the experience of love, and every other thing you think you want will miraculously appear. I know it will work because I know, as *The Course in Miracles* teaches, "The Holy Spirit will always respond to your slightest invitation."

Commentary Journal

After reading today's commentary, I realize

The key phrase(s) I want to remember and work with today are

Morning LONELINESS Affirmation

Today, I open my mind, my heart, my being to receive the flow of divine love.

I release all thoughts, doubts and fears that this is not possible.

Today, I am willing to know and experience divine love as the truth of my being.

I am love being loved.

I am an expression of all that love is.

For this I am so grateful!

And So It Is!

Let Me Remember . . .

The Holy Spirit of the Divine will respond to my slightest request.

I am an open and receptive vessel.

There is no shortage of love.

There is nothing to fear.

God's promise is to answer every request.

Urgency is a sign of being shut down.

I remember being LONELY when

I was able to overcome this experience by

I can remain open to receiving more good things I want in life by

DAY
30

When You
Feel . . . UNAPPRECIATED

Working Definition:

The emotion we are working with today is SELF-VALUE. It is diminished when we feel UNAPPRECIATED. Feeling unfulfilled in response to an action taken or gesture made outward.

Commentary on
FEELING UNAPPRECIATED

How many times have you done something for someone, or gone out of your way to do something for someone, only to have that person fail to acknowledge you? How many people have you been there for, only to find yourself alone when you need someone? How long have you worked on a job without being recognized? In how many relationships have you given your all only to be left hanging out to dry, with your broken heart on your tear-stained sleeve? If you have an answer for one or more of these scenarios, you have undoubtedly experienced feeling unappreciated. If you are anything like me, you probably get mad at the other person or people involved, and then ask yourself, "Why? Why me? Why do people ignore me? Take advantage of me?" After this useless line of questioning, I would switch gears and ask, "Why don't people appreciate what I do for them? What did I do wrong?" I found my answers in *The Course in Miracles*: "What you give to others you give to yourself." Translation: If you appreciate what you do for others, their response should be of little or no consequence to you. It took me a long time to really feel that way.

I had no idea that I was a dysfunctional person. I wasn't a bad person, I was just a little out of whack. I didn't realize I had hidden agendas, unresolved issues, unhealed wounds, or an inferiority complex. I thought I was just fine, and I set out to prove how fine I was by doing things for other people. This was long before everyone started bowing down to the god of low self-esteem. This was when people just did dysfunctional stuff that had no name, rhyme, or reason attached to it. I bought friendship with my deeds and with money. I bought affection by making myself indispensable, fulfilling any needs, and handling loose ends. I attracted attention to myself by creating drama and crisis in my life, and then getting mad at the people I had helped when they did not come to my rescue. I gave so much, to so many, and I wanted something back. I wanted a thank you. I wanted acknowledgment. I wanted people to make me feel good about me. I wanted people to recognize in me the things I could not see in myself. When they failed to meet my expectations I felt unappreciated.

"What you give to others you give to yourself." The first step toward integrating this premise into your life is the recognition of the truth that we are all alone. We are all connected to the One Life through the divine Spirit of the One Mind. There is no separation among human beings. When we understand this we realize that we are as wealthy as the one we consider the wealthiest person, as intelligent as the one we consider the most intelligent person, as beautiful as the one we consider the most beautiful person. Few dysfunctional people begin from this premise! I told myself I was okay, but I did things that supported my deepest feelings, which were that I was not okay or wealthy or intelligent, and I certainly was not beautiful. I attempted to demonstrate that I was all of those things, and when people did not applaud my demonstration with a thank you or by heaping accolades upon my person, I was crushed. Can you imagine becoming angry with a person who does not send you a thank you card when you take a cake to their home after their mother's funeral? It took me a long time to realize that most of the stuff I did for other folks, I did for recognition. It was not the doing that made me feel good; it was the compliment for the doing that I was really after. When it did not come, I feel that my efforts had not been sufficiently recognized.

I once heard the comedian Chris Rock say something that made a great deal of sense: "People always want to be rewarded for the things they are *supposed to do*." Things like showing up on time for work, or staying at work until a job is done, or taking care of the children, or being supportive or encouraging to a family member, neighbor, friend, or a spouse. You are being paid to come to work on time and to stay there until the task is complete. People who choose to become parents are responsible for providing love, guidance, and care to the children they produce. The unspoken agreement in all of our intimate relationships is to take care of (that is, love, support, and honor) one another. Every living being is accountable and responsible to their Creator to treat others in the way they would want to be treated, under all circumstances, in all situations. For these actions we should expect no rewards or recognition. It's called, "Love thy neighbor." It would be nice to be acknowledged, but it is dysfunctional to believe that people are indebted to you for what you do for them. Beneath it all is the often unrecognized, hard-to-face truth that when we expect someone else to make us feel good about what we do, chances are we have done it for the wrong reasons. There is an even better chance that we have acted with an unstated, sometimes unrecognized or dysfunctional intent. Nine out of ten of these cases are the times we feel unappreciated.

When you are trapped in this particular emotion, the only escape route is to realize that all that you have given you have received. You have served the Divine by serving one of the Divine's children who was in need. You have served yourself by sharing the bounty of grace that the Divine has provided for you. You have shared love by putting the needs of someone else before your own needs. You have opened yourself to receive the grace of divine gratitude, which promises to multiply tenfold and return to you all that you give in truth and love. When your giving and your doing for others leaves you feeling depleted and unappreciated, it is a sign of dysfunction. There is a hidden agenda lurking somewhere in the back of your mind. You must ask yourself, "Why do I want to be recognized for this thing I have done?" More important, you must ask, "How do I want to be recognized for this thing I have done?" What I discovered and used to cure my dysfunction was that when I gave something or did something with an unstated intent of making me feel good, no amount of recognition made me feel better or more appreciated. I guess it's like my mother always said, "If you have to ask for something you need, you really don't need it because God already knows your needs before you ask." The other thing I discovered about feeling unappreciated is, when I stopped expecting recognition and rewards for the things I had done, it poured in by the buckets.

Commentary Journal

After reading today's commentary, I realize

The key phrase(s) I want to remember and work with today are

Morning SELF-VALUE Affirmation

I have enough to spare.
I have enough to share.
I am enough to give to the world the best parts of me.
All that I give I give to myself.
All that I give, I give to the divine essence of myself.
All that I give is multiplied and returned to me tenfold.
For this I am so grateful.
And So It Is!

Let Me Remember . . .

All that I give, I give to myself.

All that I do, I do for myself.

When I serve others, I serve the Divine.

When I serve myself, I serve the Divine.

There is nothing I give that depletes me.

There is nothing I do that depletes me.

*The universe is an abundant environment with
enough of everything to spare.*

I am a universal being connected to all contained therein.

Evening SELF-VALUE Journal

Today, I found myself feeling UNAPPRECIATED when

I congratulate myself for not allowing myself to feel UNAPPRECIATED by

The way I can learn to give more without feeling UNAPPRECIATED is to

Phase Five

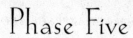

"God is not responsible for your inability to find Him."

PAUL FERRINI
Circle of Atonement

*"If you spend all your time looking for Him,
you might miss Her when She shows up."*

NEALE DONALD WALSCH
Conversations with God

Honor Your Process

The culmination of their seven-year relationship was a beautiful wedding. The second for both, but one that everyone knew was coming and would last, and one we were all happy about. They were older, more mature, wiser, and they were both on a beautiful spiritual path. He was about to retire. They were planning for their life after that. She was entering a new career and a new stage of development. She was in ministerial school. Although it meant she would be away from home, in another state, they decided it was best for her to finish so they could *really* be together. She only had one more year. A few months after the last semester began, a few months shy of their first wedding anniversary, he became very ill. It was his heart.

Two major procedures in less than two months kept her flying back and forth between school and home. She was tired. He was lonely. They had to stay on the path, keep the end in sight. Prayer got her through it. Her love and more prayer got him through it. Had either of them known it was coming, they probably would have done things a bit differently. They probably would have panicked. Maybe she would not have gone to school. Maybe he would have changed his diet long ago. Maybe they would not have gotten married. Maybe they would have saved more money. Maybe! Maybe! Maybe! Their life together was not looking the way they had pictured it. The things you worry about never seem to happen, and the things that happen unexpectedly are things you probably wouldn't have worried about. They both knew that even though they didn't know, God knew. They also knew that God would let them know what they needed to know and do when they needed to know it and do it.

Have you ever asked yourself why the road curves? Why can't all roads be straight? Why do city streets go up and down or around corners? My friend Joie asked me this question in the midst of one of my life crises when I was beating up on myself. Why didn't I see it coming? How come I didn't recognize this before now? "Because," Joie said, "you would not have been able to handle it before now." That's why the road curves. It provides us with the opportunity to take in a little at a time. As we move forward, covering more ground, a little more is revealed to us. That's how life works. It gives you what you can handle in small doses, even when you think you are able to handle more. It is called the grace of God.

There was a time in my life when I was never good enough, right enough, smart enough, for me. There was always something wrong with me or what I had done. There was always more I should have done, someplace else I should have been. I never seemed to get it quite right for my tastes. In other words, I was always complaining about something. The glass was always half empty. I can now accept and understand how my complaining got on everyone's nerves, including my own. I would hear myself say things and then I would beat up on myself for saying them. I didn't trust myself. I didn't like myself. And on a bad day, I will slip right back into those old patterns. Today, however, I have one saving grace. I realize that no matter how much is in the glass, it is for that time, in that moment, as full as it is going to get.

Wherever you find yourself is exactly where you need to be. Even when you want to be somewhere else, under different circumstances, life knows that you probably could not handle it. Deepak Chopra wrote, "Whatever relationships you have attracted into your life at any given time, are the relationships you need to be in at that time." When you are ready to do a new thing, in a new way, you will do it, with new people. There are people waiting for who you are becoming. Chances are, you are not ready to meet them today. At every given moment, we are each in the process of being and becoming. We are taking in as much as we can. The road is curved, and we are being prepared to handle what is waiting around the bend.

Webster defines "process" as a natural phenomena marked by gradual changes that lead toward a particular result. That is a very apt description of life. We experience a little and change. We discover a little more about life, ourselves, and people, and change some more. The result we are seeking is remembering who we are. In order to remember that, we must know who we are not. Life is the process of recognizing who we are not. Each time we face a challenge, obstacle, or difficulty, we learn what we can and cannot do. No matter what we do, it is the best we can do under the given circumstances with the information we have at the time. I could never get that quite right. I always thought I should have done or should be doing something else. I forgot about the process.

The conditions we face do not define us. They remind us of who we are and who we want to be. When I was in an abusive marriage I knew that was not what I wanted. I knew I had no business being there. The experience taught me that I am not here to be beaten. The experiences we encounter are not who we are. They do, however, remind us of what we are thinking about ourselves. If we think we should be punished, we will be. If we think we can be attacked, we will be. Each of us is in the process of remembering that we are divine, miraculous, powerful manifestations of life. We learn the truth of this each time we fall down and get up, experience loss and recover, make a choice and change our minds. Every experience moves us a little further along life's road and around its curves.

If I had known at age nineteen that my marriage would be violent, it would have devastated me. I could not have handled it, and I probably would have ignored the information. If I had known on Tuesday that my mother was going to die on Thursday, I would not have made it to her funeral. I would have been in the nuthouse! If I had known that my one and only son was headed for three and a half years in prison, I would have stopped breathing long before he went. Thank you, God, for making curves in the road! Thank you for loving us enough to give just what we can handle, when we can handle it! Thank you, God, for allowing the process of life to be a slow and gentle course in memory development. I, for one, am not sure I could handle knowing just how magnificent I am all at once!

DAY
31

Honor Your Process
with . . . AUTHENTICITY

Working Definition:

The principle we are working with today is AUTHENTICITY. *It is real. Actual. Made as same as the original. Natural outgrowth of the master. Conforming to or based on truth or essence of original.*

Commentary on AUTHENTICITY

What kind of games do you play? The question did not strike me as odd at first. My perfectly logical brain went to the perfectly logical response, "I really like Monopoly, but I rarely get a chance to play it, with work and all, you know. I'm really busy!" *What kind of games do you play?* This time it hit me in the face like a bucket of cold water. His voice was lower, his eyes piercing; his manner said that he knew and that I had better 'fess up. Why is it that when you need your brain it goes to the mall? I knew exactly what he was talking about; however, my lips and my tongue were out at Nordstrom's trying to get coordinated. Fear, shame, and guilt were throwing sand in my eyes. I couldn't breathe. *What kind of games do you play?* In the absence of my brain and tongue, I did what any "found out" person would do. I cried.

I wanted to write a book entitled *Divas Don't Fart: 101 Creative Ways Humans Disguise Their Mistakes.* My theory is that most people go to extraordinary means to cover up the fact that they fart. We will squeeze the cheeks of the behind together, hoping the fart won't make noise. We will fart and move away, hoping the odor does not follow us. I myself have let out a whooper and then darted my eyes around the room in an accusatory manner or said out loud, "Boy, what is that smell?" I believe there is a little diva in everyone. The diva is always perfect and infallible. The diva is above reproach. The diva would not dare do something so common as farting. To fart is to be fallible. Meaning, you can make a mistake. Divas don't make mistakes. Unfortunately, what the diva does not realize is that mistakes are natural occurrences. They are an outgrowth of the consequences of the natural flow of life. They may not be appealing or pleasant, but mistakes are as natural as farts. They are authentic. When the diva in us refuses to acknowledge the natural and common outgrowths of our actions in life, we resort to playing games. I confess. I was guilty of being a game-playing diva, and I was caught.

What kind of games do you play? I played the *I Don't Know Game*. As long as I didn't know, I could not be wrong. I played the *Money Game*. I didn't have the money to do what I needed to do. As long as I could not do something, I could not fail at doing it. I also used the money game as an excuse not to keep my agreements. I would borrow money and not pay it back as agreed. This would usually make somebody real mad. Why are you mad at me? I don't have any money! At that point I could get mad at other people for being mad at me because I did not have the money to give back, as agreed. This was actually a disguised version of the *See What They Are Doing to Me Game*. I was a lifelong victim of somebody; my parents, my husband, the people from whom I had borrowed money were all doing something bad to me. As long as I was a victim of what somebody else was doing to me, it was not necessary to own up to what I was doing to myself or anyone else.

The most elaborate and complex game of all was the *I Can't Take It Anymore Game*. This is where you take on more than you can humanly do or want to do, fail to complete what you start, create all sorts of chaos in your life, and then complain about how much people expect of you. These games were the outgrowths of the fear of being disapproved, fed by the fear of not being accepted, laced with the fear of not doing it right, stewed in the belief that I was not good enough. Covering all of this was the flamboyance of the *I-can-do-no-wrong-diva* in me. I did not fart. Translation, I was not authentic.

In order to be authentic, you must be willing to acknowledge and accept the natural outgrowths of everything you think, do, and say in this life. In other words, you must be willing to fart in public. People around you are merely mirrors of the various aspects of yourself. They will say what you think. They will do what you are afraid of doing or of having done to you. There is nothing in your life but you and God. Anything that shows up is either a reflection of God or a reflection of you. When people in your world act ugly or do ugly things, it is a reflection of some part of you. Resist the temptation to get mad at them. Don't act like you do not know what is going on or why it is going on in your world. Search your heart and mind for the mistake in thought, word, or deed that has shown up in your life as a fart.

Authenticity also requires that you stay in touch with your feelings. You cannot deny what you feel, and you cannot hold it back. Be authentic! Learn how to describe and communicate what you are feeling when you feel it, first to yourself. You can communicate with others as necessary. In much the same way that we do not like to fart, we do not like to feel, particularly when the feeling makes us uncomfortable. Feelings make you authentic. They make you different from everyone else. Most important, feelings let you know you are alive. If you want to live an authentic life, free from the demands of the diva in you, you must allow yourself to feel.

Another important aspect of being authentic is the willingness to always tell the truth. Gay and Kathlyn Hendricks call it "the microscopic truth." This means telling the truth about every little thing. When you fart, don't blame someone else, own it! When you hurt, don't say it's okay. Own your pain. Own your fear. Own everything you create, internally and externally. Acknowledge every emotion for exactly what it is, a part of you. It deserves the same recognition that you do. When you own what you feel, you are empowered to make a conscious choice about how to change the feeling. When other people know what you feel, you are empowered to both create and define boundaries. Authenticity also demands no comparison. You cannot compare yourself or what you do to anyone else. You are you! You represent a true and original part of the Master. There is no one else like you. Author Og Mandino has called you "the greatest miracle in the world." To the degree that you compare yourself to others and govern your actions by the actions of others, you will be lost.

Finally and most important of all, authenticity means that you must do what you do the way you do it and allow everyone else the same courtesy. There was a time I wanted to be like every famous writer that ever lived. I tried to copy styles, reframe information, use similar artwork. I almost drove myself crazy! Now I just do what I do. I have mentors. There are people whose work I admire, but I write the way I write. I eat the way I eat. I dress the way I dress. I can't believe that God made us each so unique only to have us do everything the same way. When we each live up to our authentic selves, we can all do the same thing and not flood the market. When we each own the parts of ourselves that are authentic, we can entertain, support, educate, and heal one another in perpetuity. When we each own our farts, we work toward eliminating prejudice, oppression, and hate. The more games we play, the more rules we are required to follow. The more rules there are, the less opportunities there are for creativity. Creativity needs authenticity. Without it, the Master in you cannot truly be recognized or glorified.

Commentary Journal

After reading today's commentary, I realize

The key phrase(s) I want to remember and work with today are

Morning AUTHENTICITY Affirmation

There is no one on the planet exactly like me.
I am an original.
I am AUTHENTIC.
I am one of a kind, alive to offer a unique and special gift.
I am an AUTHENTIC imprint, alive to show the world is a unique
  representation of God.
I am as God created me to be.
I am AUTHENTIC!
I am original!
I am divine!
For this I am so grateful.
And So It Is!

Let Me Remember . . .

There is no one else on earth exactly like me.

I am a unique expression of the original Master.

Mistakes are natural occurrences.

No one else can do what I have been born to do.

I cannot do what someone else was born to do.

I am as God created me to be.

Evening AUTHENTICITY Journal

I congratulate myself for remaining my AUTHENTIC self when

Instead of playing these games, I can be AUTHENTIC by

I now understand I cannot be AUTHENTIC when

DAY
32

Honor Your Process
with . . . PATIENCE

Working Definition:

Demonstration of steadfastness and assurance. The principle we are work-ing with today is PATIENCE. It is stability. A mental attitude of calm and poise. The foundation of faith.

Commentary on PATIENCE

Most of us have very little trouble identifying what it is that we want in life. The difficulty we experience is in waiting for what we want to manifest as a tangible condition. Waiting takes patience, and it is a virtue most of us do not possess. Patience requires faith. Faith demands trust. In order to trust, you must know the truth. The truth is usually relative to our experiences. When you explore and understand the elements required to actually demonstrate patience, it is probably safe to say that a large majority of us are in a great deal of trouble when it comes to having patience. Without patience, we worry, we complain, and sometimes we give up hope. We do not understand that a delay is not a denial, and that if we faithfully trust the truth, we would find it is a lot less difficult to employ patience.

I was rushing around the house trying to get somewhere I should have been, looking for pantyhose while putting on eyeliner, ironing my blouse while brushing my teeth. It is amazing the number of things you can do when you are late. I was just about to put on my lipstick when the tele-phone rang. Why is it that the telephone always rings when you are late? Something said to me, "Don't answer that!" Did I listen? Of course not!

"Hello." It was my son. My only son. Calling collect from God's vacation retreat center, commonly called prison. "I'll accept." "Ma!" "Yes, son of mine." "I'm in trouble!" "That's obvious! You are in prison!" "No, Ma! I mean I'm in trouble in prison." "Damon, I've got to be out of this house fifteen minutes ago. Talk fast!" It was 2:30 in the afternoon, the hour of the highest telephone rates. I was angry with myself for piddling around so long that I had made myself late. In the midst of it all my son was calling and needing to engage in a heart-to-heart, mother-to-son conversation. I was late and this telephone call was interfering with my plans! I think I was becoming a bit impatient.

He had lent another inmate his favorite Charlie Brown book. That inmate lent the book to another inmate. When he went to retrieve his book from still another inmate, that inmate was reading it and refused to give it to him. He admitted that he was having a bad hair day. He became so furious with the inmate he hit him. The other inmate hit him back. Soon several inmates were pummeling him. In an attempt to save himself, he sunk his teeth into somebody's chest, dragged the man over to the door of the room, wrestled his way free from all the fists and feet that were upon him, and ran away to call me. "Oh, Lord!" Then he went on to say, "Ma, I've been doing everything you told me. I have been reading and praying and meditating. I have been breathing and forgiving and praising. I have been thinking positive thoughts, speaking positive words, doing positive things, and you know what, Ma? It ain't working!"

The greatest challenge to the development of patience is being able to wait for the tangible evidence that your efforts are paying off. We have a fixed idea of what we want and what it will look like when it shows up. We hold that idea so firmly that often we are unable to detect that the very thing we want has actually arrived. If it does not look the way we thought it would, or if it does not feel the way we imagined it would, we are unable to detect its presence. Discernment is an important part of patience. We must be able to see through the appearances, and be able to recognize the manifestation of our desires. This requires an inner knowing. That knowing is called patience.

"Ma, you told me that if I expect the best I would get it. You told me whatever I asked in faith, believing I would have it, I would have it. I have been up for parole twice, each time believing I would be able to come home. Each time, my parole has been denied. This stuff doesn't work! It just doesn't work, Ma!" I was going to be very, very late. He rambled on for a few more minutes about the conditions of his living environment, about the undesirable nature of those among whom he lived, the unloving attitudes of those in charge of his living environment, and he concluded by saying, "God does not work in the prison!" I was going to be very, very, very late!

I knew the truth, and it was time for my son to know it. I had total and complete trust in the wisdom of the Divine, believing that my only son was in prison learning a powerful lesson about choices and responsibility. I had total, complete, unshakeable faith that even though I did not like the fact that my son was in prison, there was a greater good that had to manifest as a result. All I needed was the patience to sit down for five minutes and share with him what I knew and believed. I took a deep breath, placed my shoes on the kitchen table, and reminded my son of the following things:

1. You are going to be tested by fire. Each time you make a choice, you must be prepared to experience the consequence of that choice. Most of us are aware of some of the consequences. However, there are always things that we do not know and cannot see. When these unknown, unseen consequences show themselves in our lives, we must be steadfast, believing in the wisdom of the spiritual laws of the universe, knowing that the best is yet to come. You must have trust and be patient.

2. You must not allow the wind to rattle your core. A hard-blowing wind will rip the leaves from the branches. It will cause the weak limbs of a tree to snap. It may even cause some pretty large branches to snap off. A wind, however, cannot affect the core, the inner essence of a sturdy tree. A strong wind cannot disturb the dark, peaceful calm at the bottom of the ocean. What is at your core that would allow you to drag a man around in your teeth over a Charlie Brown book? Has your praying, meditating, and breathing just been lip service? When a gusty wind blows through your life, you must retreat to your core. You must not break. You must have faith and be patient.

3. Spirit and things of a spiritual nature do not work on your schedule. The fact that you have a schedule, the fact that you want certain things to occur, in a certain way, at a certain time, is an indication that you believe you are in control, that you believe the spirit of life must answer to you. You are not in control! You are in a process of spiritual unfolding, and in that process, whether you like it or not, spirit will use every experience possible to ensure that your development is on schedule—a spiritual schedule. You cannot watch the clock or the calendar. You must watch your heart, know the truth, and be patient with your unfolding process.

I could barely hear him breathing on the other end of the telephone. I explained to him that patience is more than the ability to wait at the bus stop for forty-five minutes. It is so much more than being able to control several four-year-olds while watching the evening news. Patience is a demonstration of your willingness to surrender total and complete control to the wisdom of God. It is the ability to discern the unfolding of a goal in the midst of a windstorm. It is knowing that your efforts are paying off even when there is no tangible evidence to support that belief. Patience is being able to retreat to your core when you are being challenged and pull up everything in your arsenal of truth that will glorify the presence of the Divine in your being. Patience is knowing that you have done your best, and that what will be on the test is what you already know.

I realized I was really talking to myself. The day had unfolded according to a divine plan. I was at home because I needed to be at home when my son called. There was no need to rush or beat up on myself. There was something much greater than my plan at work here, and I was being called to surrender to it. I realized that the only thing I was missing at the luncheon was a welcome address and a wilted salad. I did not need to risk a speeding ticket for either of those. As the thoughts raced through my mind, I heard my son say, "I'm really not ready to come home yet, am I? I still have some work to do on me, on my faith and discipline." With all the love and patience I could muster at the moment, I responded, "Son of mine, you don't have to get an A on life's tests; you only have to pass. You took the time to call rather than stay in the middle of a brawl. If you ask me, I think you are doing just fine."

Commentary Journal

After reading today's commentary, I realize

The key phrase(s) I want to remember and work with today are

Morning PATIENCE Affirmation

I move in time according to divine order.
I am where I need to be, when I need to be there, doing what I need to do,
when I need to be doing it.
The divine order of divine time guides my steps, my manner, and my life.
I move in time according to divine order.
I move in time according to divine order.
I move in time according to divine order.
For this I am so grateful!
And So It Is!

Let Me Remember . . .

Trust, truth, and faith are the foundation of patience.

For everything, there is a season.

I am not in control.

A strong wind cannot disturb my core.

Divine time and divine order are guarantees of my divine good.

There is more than I can see going on.

Evening PATIENCE Journal

I congratulate myself for being PATIENT today when

I find that I become impatient with others when

I realize I have not been PATIENT with myself about

DAY
33

Honor Your Process
with . . . FAITH

Working Definition:

The principle we are working with today is FAITH. It is the magnetic pull of the heart's desire. An inner knowing that brings spiritual/emotional assurance. The substance/foundation of that which one believes.

Commentary on FAITH

Faith is not something we must acquire or develop. Faith is something we have by virtue of being alive. I once thought that I had to work to make my faith stronger. This is a favorite doctrine of organized religion. "Keep your faith strong." "Make your faith work for you." Like many people, I thought faith was something that came and went according to your ability to adhere to certain regimented practices. The more you pray, the stronger your faith will become. The more fellowship you have with like-minded people, the greater your faith will be. These concepts and practices will take you only so far. What I discovered is that faith is the result of your knowledge and unwavering belief in the perfect operation of spiritual laws. When you know and understand the laws of the spiritual universe, you have faith that they will work on your behalf. When you do not know spiritual law, you place your faith in the belief that something or someone can cause something to happen or keep it from happening. Most of my attempts to be or become more faithful gave way to doubt. Doubt is the result of ignorance of the spiritual laws. I didn't believe I was doing the right things in the right way to "make" what I wanted to happen, happen. When you understand spiritual law, you come to know that the laws work just because they work, not because you must apply them in a particularly correct way.

We all have faith. No one person has more faith than the other. What some of us have been able to do is to master the ability to place our faith in appropriate things, those things that we want to see manifest in our lives. On the other hand, some of us place our faith in the expectation of the worst possible event taking place. It's called worry. We worry about our safety. We worry about our children. We worry about money. Worry is placing faith in inappropriate thoughts of undesirable expectations. Those who have mastered faith place their thoughts on the goodness and all-sufficiency of the Divine. They keep their minds focused on truth. They intend and expect to experience the best of everything, all the time. These people have no more information than you or I. They do, however, understand that the power of their minds will attract the exact reflection of their most dominant thought. They have surrendered their human will to the will of the Holy Spirit because they realize good is the activity of the Holy Spirit. They understand that they cannot have a desire that will remain unfulfilled if that desire is part of the Divine's plan for their life. Those who have mastered the principle of faith further understand that they are creating their world with thought, word, and deed. Consequently they know that if they are working toward their greater good, if they are working up to their highest capability, if they are honoring themselves and those around them, the laws of the universe must work in their behalf. This knowing is called faith.

Most of us know the "faith quotes" verbatim. "If you have faith the size of a mustard seed . . . " "Keep the faith!" "Faith is the substance of things hoped for . . . " "If you have faith, you can say to the mountain . . . " I don't know about you, but I have not talked to any mountains lately! I have been too busy worrying about what is going to happen, when it is going to happen, and what will happen to me if this or that happens. "O ye of little faith!" Although we each go to bed at night without questioning whether or not we will get up the next morning, we still don't get it. Laying down to sleep, inhaling and exhaling, raising your hand to the tip of your nose, all are examples of faith. We have unquestionable faith that we will be able to do the things we want to do when we want to do them. The challenge we face is developing a "living faith." The faith in our ability and right to live fuller, richer, more meaningful lives all of the time.

You are faith in the flesh. God has so much faith in you that you were entrusted with the gift of life and a unique mission to fulfill. Did you ever stop to think that you could have been a fruit tree. You could have berries or flowers sticking out of your ears! Instead you were given the right to make conscious choices, the ability to create through thought and deed, and dominion over every other creature. That is a demonstration of the faith the Divine has in your abilities and capabilities. Your task is to return faith with faith. You must live with the knowledge that everything you need, at any time you need it, *is being* provided. Not *will be* provided. *Is being provided!* This is how we can each become an example of living faith: by knowing that your good is on the way. In every undertaking you must live with faith in the power of your thoughts, the efficacy of your words, and the purposefulness of your actions. When you are challenged by seemingly insurmountable obstacles, you must live with faith that the truth of your affirmations, your positive words, will manifest as tangible conditions. When you set a goal, you must proceed with living faith that there is a divine plan unfolding in your life and as your life, and that if the plan is supported by knowledge of spiritual laws, the benefits will be divine. This is how we must direct our thoughts and actions in order to become living faith.

There is one important aspect of living faith and having faith of which we must always remain conscious. Faith will not get you anything you want! It will bring you to the realization and living experience of what is divinely ordained for you and what you create through your divine identity. For example, let's say you want to be a singer, but you have a horrible voice. I'm not talking about singing a little off-key. I mean, a voice that curdles milk and frightens babies! You know you sound terrible, but you've got your heart set on being a Grammy Award–winning singer. Please be advised: There is no amount of faith in the world that can make that happen. It is not spiritually appropriate to put your faith in something that is beyond your level of skill and capability. On the other hand, you may have a beautiful voice, you may want to be a singer, but you cannot get a job as a singing waiter or waitress. Will faith help you? Perhaps. The entire matter will turn on your intent and expectation. Do you want to sing just to make money? Do you want to sing because you have faith in your ability and your desire to share your gift? Do you want to sing because you love to sing? Spiritual law says, "What you give, you get!" When you give with good intentions, you reap good results. When you give with love, you reap what you give tenfold.

Some of us want things for reasons that are not in alignment with spiritual law or our spiritual purpose. Many people have been disappointed when the things they ask for in faith fail to manifest. The issue is, was there living faith behind your request? Or was there fear? Fear that it couldn't happen or wouldn't happen for you will assassinate every shred of faith you have. The other big issue we must address is, is what you are asking for in alignment with your spiritual purpose? Often we pray, plead, beg for what we want to become a reality. Praying, begging, or pleading with God is not a show of faith. It is an attempt to impose your will onto the will of the Divine. Surrender is faith's older brother. In order for living faith to manifest as a tangible experience, you must surrender fear, doubt, worry. Most important of all, you must surrender your will, knowing that the will of the Divine is your salvation.

The only requirement for you to become a living example of faith is to work on yourself. Work on expanding your knowledge of and ability to embrace truth. Work on your acknowledgment and acceptance of your true identity as a child of the Divine. Work on eliminating every thought, idea, belief, and judgment that supports the belief that you are separate from God and unworthy of God's good. As you begin to work on you and expand your awareness of spiritual law, your willingness to trust in the wisdom of the Divine will become your overcoat and the ever-present grace of the Divine will become your best friend. With trust, truth, and grace on your side, faith will be your claim to fame.

Commentary Journal

After reading today's commentary, I realize

The key phrase(s) I want to remember and work with today are

Morning FAITH Affirmation

I am the walking, talking, living embodiment of FAITH.
I breathe in FAITH.
I live through FAITH.
I see everything through FAITH-filled eyes.
I speak with FAITH.
I listen in FAITH.
I know that FAITH can, when I cannot!
I know that FAITH is always, under all circumstances, and in all
   situations, the blessed activity of the Holy Spirit moving in my life.
For this I am so grateful!
And So It Is!

Let Me Remember . . .

God has FAITH in me.

I am living FAITH.

Spiritual law works on behalf of those who live in FAITH.

Conscious thought, powerful words, purposeful deeds are proof of my
FAITH.

FAITH can when I cannot.

Surrender is FAITH's big brother.

God's grace is FAITH'S mother.

Trust is the key to FAITH.

FAITH ignites the activity of the HOLY SPIRIT.

Evening FAITH Journal

I congratulate myself for being able to demonstrate FAITH today when

The challenge I faced today that tested my FAITH was

I am willing to employ greater FAITH in my approach to

DAY
34

Honor Your Process with . . . Discipline

Working Definition:

The principle we are working with today is DISCIPLINE. It is an orderly or prescribed conduct or pattern of behavior. Training or instruction that perfects or molds mental faculties and moral character.

Commentary on DISCIPLINE

There is no getting around doing what you need to do. You can avoid or postpone any task for any length of time. However, when it comes to doing something that you need to do, you will either do it or reap the consequences of not doing it. The consequences can be harsh and unpleasant. The consequences also seem to follow a general rule: the longer you avoid or postpone, the more harsh and/or unpleasant a task will be. When you know there is something you need to do, the best thing to do is to do it. In order to do whatever it is requires that you have discipline. When God was giving out discipline, I must have been at the mall!

When I first noticed that my tooth was becoming sensitive to hot and cold, I was not disciplined enough to call the dentist. Two root canals and $600 later, I recognized the value of discipline. When my ex-husband started coming in late, which evolved into staying out all night, two and three nights in a row, I practiced the speech I would give him at least twenty times a day, for at least twenty months. Did I have the discipline to say what I needed to say, ask what I told myself I would ask? Of course not! Two babies, two broken ribs, and a wired jaw later, I actually understood the value of discipline. When dragging my body out of the bed, in order to drag it to a job I hated, was not enough evidence that I needed to move beyond fear by disciplining myself and my life in order to pursue my heart's desire, getting fired for being late and demonstrating a "lackluster" performance provided all the evidence I needed. In essence, discipline is having the courage to do what needs to be done before you are forced to do it.

I once heard Oprah Winfrey say, "Discipline comes from doing!" I was very sad to know that. I thought I could keep praying for discipline, keep reading about discipline, keep hoping that one day I would wake up and find I had been advanced to the head of the discipline line. It was quite disconcerting to discover that the only way I would develop the discipline to do what I kept avoiding was by doing the very thing I kept avoiding. Somehow that just doesn't seem quite fair! Besides that, when I think about why I was avoiding certain things (TRUST!), how hard the things I avoided appeared to be (WILLING-NESS!), and how many other things demanded my attention at the same time (CHOICE!), I concluded that the doing aspect of discipline was more than I could handle.

How many diets had I started and not finished? How many morning exercise and meditation schedules had I developed? How many promises had I made with myself that I had failed to keep? How many times did I wait until the last minute to do something and suffer the hysteria of working under stress? How many times had I promised not to say or do something only to find myself embroiled in chaos or controversy because I did or said what I had told myself I would not do or say? I did not understand why my grandmother insisted that I make my bed before I brushed my teeth, or why she insisted that I iron all the clothes I planned to wear during the week on Saturday morning. It made absolutely no sense to me that I had to wash my hair every Tuesday, polish the silver every Wednesday, eat my vegetables before I ate the meat, or put the rollers in the back of my head before I put them in the top. My grandmother was a stickler for doing everything in a particular way at a certain time, and as a result she usually got quite a bit done. My grandmother was very disciplined. I, on the other hand, was not.

What I have learned after many painful experiences, resulting from years of avoidance and procrastination, is that when you begin to honor yourself and your life, you become disciplined about how you handle yourself and your life. Beyond the realm of just *doing,* discipline is *attending to* with care. When you feel good about yourself, you attend to your care in a gentle and disciplined manner. When you honor the gift of life, you attend to the affairs of life with a disciplined approach. When you accept and acknowledge that you and your life are part of a loving process, you are eager to be an active participant. You realize that all that you do, and the manner in which you do it, will determine how far you go and how quickly the process will move forward. Discipline is not easy, but it is a necessary skill to develop, the only real demonstration of the value you place on yourself, and the reason you have been placed on the planet.

Commentary Journal

After reading today's commentary, I realize

The key phrase(s) I want to remember and work with today are

Morning DISCIPLINE Affirmation

I love myself enough to attend to myself with DISCIPLINE and care.
I love life enough to attend to the affairs of my life in a DISCIPLINED way.
I love God enough to attend to myself and my life with DISCIPLINE and care.
God loves me enough to show me the areas of my life in which I need to employ more DISCIPLINE.
I am willing!
I am receptive!
For this I am so grateful!
And So It Is!

Let Me Remember . . .

Discipline comes from doing.

Discipline is how I honor myself.

Discipline is how I honor my life.

Discipline is how I honor the Divine.

Discipline eliminates stress.

I congratulate myself for showing DISCIPLINE today when

I realize I still need more DISCIPLINE as it relates to

The benefits I can look forward to as a result of employing more DISCIPLINE are

Phase Six

Just as the spider unfolds its web
from within its own being,
we must unfold divine wisdom, divine joy
and the divine potential of God from within ourselves.
The moment we stop trying to make God come to us,
we will realize that God is already here.

JOEL GOLDSMITH
In *A Parenthesis in Eternity*

Honor Life

I have often been ashamed of myself and my life. I have done some things that I considered inexcusable and unforgivable. I have many times, in many ways, put myself in jeopardy. I have been defiant, and at times I thought I had been defeated. I finally realized nothing I had done had anything to do with life. It was all a big misunderstanding. I did not understand what life was really about. I did not understand my role in life. I did not know how to honor myself, and I did not know it was necessary to honor life. I was confused and clueless until the day I asked to die. I got down on my knees and prayed to God to take my life. I had already failed at two suicide attempts, so I wasn't going that route again. I just didn't want to be on the planet, and since I knew that God had placed me here, I was begging Him to let me leave. I prayed, and I cried for hours. When I finished, I was still alive. A few days later, I was watching an evangelist on television. In the middle of his sermon, he pointed his finger outward and said, "God does want your life! He gave it to you! Honor what God has given you and do something with your life!" It was exactly what I needed to hear, but I didn't know where to begin.

Life is a process of growing, outgrowing, and growing some more. There was a time when I thought life was hard work. Now I know that it is a process of total surrender. In order to live fully, we are required to grow into our divine potential by outgrowing our thoughts of limitation. Each experience we live through and grow through is a vitally important aspect of spiritual growth. These steps ultimately enable us to outgrow those things we believed to be right, wrong, good, bad, necessary, and unnecessary. The only way we can grow into our divine identity is to live through and outgrow the limitations we place on ourselves. It feels like work. It looks like work. It is, however, a divinely guided growth process.

The ancient mystery schools taught that if you can define a thing, you don't understand it. How can you define life? What adjectives, verbs, flowering descriptions could you offer to provide an adequate description for the divine process of growing and outgrowing? What would you say if a Martian were standing before you today, asking, "What is this thing called life?" How would you describe it? How could you give this alien being a full understanding of the essence of life? I would not know where to begin. I do not know what words I would use. I would be dumbfounded, just as I am most of the time about the miraculous process called life.

"Go with the flow!" "Roll with the punches!" "Take each day as it comes!" If you are still alive, it means you do not know the whole story. Each of us must wait until the final outcome. To honor life, we must be willing to grow through what we don't know yet, and outgrow what we know no longer fits us. To honor life, we must be willing to give in to the process, moment by moment, realizing a new plot may be unfolding, a new character may be about to take the stage. In honoring life, we must give credit to the divine director, producer, and creator of this live production, by acknowledging and accepting that He knows the final outcome and the role we must play. The Divine will help us develop our character. The Divine will unveil the twisting, turning plot of the story and make sure that we are not upstaged. The Divine will honor us by protecting us as we grow. In order to honor life and its director, we must only show up, stay alert, and be willing to learn the part.

DAY 35

Honor Life
with . . . Balance

Working Definition:

The principle we are working with today is BALANCE. It is a state of being in proportion, one thing to another. To arrange so that one set of elements equals another.

Commentary on BALANCE

Rest. Work. Play. Serve. Learn. Teach. Give. Receive. A little bit of this. A little bit of that. Stop. Go. Speak. Listen. Cry a little. Understand more. Pray a lot. Rejoice even more. No matter who you are and what you think you know or do not know, life will teach you to honor and respect balance. There must be discords in order to achieve harmony. There must be darkness that propels us into light. It is the frigid cold that teaches us to appreciate the warmth. Anyone who has ever been an underdog knows about the upper hand. Whether we consciously strive to attain it or in reflection realize it has been inflicted upon us, balance is the order of the day, and all the smart people seek to balance their days. Now, I don't know about you, but I have not been a smart person most of my life. I admit that for most of my life, I have been totally out of balance, but it wasn't my fault!

As a very young child, I learned to measure my worth in proportion to what I did rather than who I was. The more I did, the more valuable I felt. The more valuable I felt, the more I sought to do. I was a do-more-better doing kind of person. You would think that I would at least be smart enough to do what I enjoyed doing. Oh, no! Not me! Do-more-better people evolve into do-more-better-faster people, which makes the doing a chore. It is work. Hard work! Trust me, do-more-better-faster people like the kind I was do not enjoy working; we simply do not know how to stop. Eventually even the fun stuff becomes work. You work from sunup to sundown, afraid to stop, afraid to lose your worth in the eyes of others. But, more important, you are afraid that the moment you stop doing, you will lose the worth and value you have placed on yourself. It is this do-more-better-faster approach to living that leads to physical, mental, emotional, and spiritual imbalance. It's pretty rough on your feet and legs too!

I think my brother contributed to my imbalance by constantly saying to me, "You play too much!" I know my teachers contributed by telling me, "You don't study enough!" My mother, bless her heart, made the most valuable contribution of all when she said, "You just don't know what to do with yourself, do you?" She was right! I didn't know what to do, or how much of it to do. I knew that hard work would bring me monetary rewards. I knew that serious study would bring me academic honors. I also knew that playing, relaxing, or just having fun would take precious time away from the hard work and study that would bring me more rewards. Yet, it seemed to me that the harder I worked, the more resentful I became. The more I studied, the more obsessive I became. I was getting nowhere, real fast, because I was broke, tired, hostile, and very, very bitchy, until a dear friend taught me about balance.

Life, she said, has many avenues, and you owe it to your shoes to spend a little time on each and every avenue. How, she asked, do you expect to know what is going on and the benefits of strolling down the avenues if you take only one road, one path, one street all of the time? There are days, she told me, when you must stroll down the avenue barefoot. There will be times, she said, when you must prance down the avenue in your high-heeled shoes. If, she explained, you want to know what is *really happening* on the avenue, you must put on your busted-up sneakers and hang out with the folks. Don't forget, she warned me, to be present on the avenue when all of the other penny loafers are out strolling too. Then, she said, there are those special occasions, those very special times, when you must put on your gold lamé slippers and glide down the avenue observing all of the things you probably missed all of the other times. Above all else, my friend explained, you must know what shoes to wear and what avenue to stroll if you want to discover the best of life. What she said sounded very nice, almost poetic, but WHAT THE HECK DID IT HAVE TO DO WITH MY FEELING THE NEED TO WORK ALL THE TIME?!!

Balance. Take time to play in your bare feet. It will keep you connected to the glorious nature and the innocence of the child within. Put on your high-heeled pumps or shiny black spats, and go dancing every now and again. It will keep you in touch with the rhythm of life. Reach back, reach out, to help somebody, sometime. When you are reaching back, out, or down, you are serving. When you serve, do it with humility. Sneakers with holes in them are a symbol of humility. You are a student of life. There is always something new for you to learn each day. Every good student knows that penny loafers are essential to higher learning. There are times when you must sit down and commune. Commune with nature, with your inner self, and with God. Gold lamé slippers are an essential part of communion. They are a gentle reminder that "the ground upon which you stand is holy ground." When you look down and see gold lamé slippers on your feet, chills of worth and value run up and down your spine. You become grateful to be alive, and because you are alive, you want to savor all of the experiences of every aspect of life.

Balance is key to your ability to savor life. Balance does not require you to do anything better or faster than anyone else. It requires only that you make a conscious effort to enjoy what you are doing, and that you learn to be present in every aspect of life, for some portion of each day that you are alive. Rest. Work. Play. Serve. Learn. Teach. Give. Receive. A little bit of this. A little bit of that. Stop. Go. Speak. Listen. Cry some more. Understand some more. Pray some more. Rejoice even more. Balance is the key to enlightenment. Enlightenment is the key to self-value and self-worth. An enlightened person with a solid sense of value and worth owns many kinds of shoes, and wears them at the appropriate times in order to walk, stroll, run, hop, skip, and dance down the many wonderful avenues of life.

After reading today's commentary, I realize

The key phrase(s) I want to remember and work with today are

Morning BALANCE Affirmation

I live a BALANCED life.
I take time to work and time to play.
I take time to learn and time to teach.
I take time to give, and I am open to receiving
  the bountiful blessings of life.
I spend time with myself.
I spend time with the Divine.
I spend time with others.
I spend time in nature.
I take the time to spend time, enjoying all that life has to offer.
I live a BALANCED life.
For this I am so grateful.
And So It Is!

Let Me Remember . . .

Rest. Work. Play. Serve. Learn. Teach. Give. Receive.

Life is a wonderful place with many things to do and many things to learn.
My worth is not attached to what I do.

There is a child in me who loves to play.

There is a growing being within me who needs to rest.

Chords and discords create harmony in the balance of life.

Evening BALANCE Journal

Today, I celebrate myself for creating BALANCE by

Today, I found it difficult to achieve BALANCE because

Today, I realized I felt out of balance when/because

DAY
36

Honor Life
. . . with EXPANSION

Working Definition:

The principle we are working with today is EXPANSION. It is the process of increasing volume, territory, and dimension. Growth. A natural evolutionary process.

Commentary on EXPANSION

My grandmother called it daydreaming. Shakti Gawain wrote a book about it called *Creative Visualization*. Rev. Michael Beckwith, of the Agape Church of Religious Science, calls it visioning. I've taken to calling it getting clear, getting on purpose, and doing God's will. Whatever we call it, however we choose to do it, ultimately it boils down to growing beyond where we are. The big question is how do you do it? How do you grow into your full potential? I have asked that question of myself and others, in a variety of ways, on a number of occasions. At various times I've gotten different answers. The one answer that had the greatest impact was something to the effect of, *"God wants only the best for you and only God knows what the best for you is."*

It is sometimes very difficult to see yourself beyond where you are in this moment. It is even more challenging to figure out how you will get there. Daydreaming or visualizing is one of the many possible ways to expand the view of your life. Unfortunately, Grandma warned me about daydreaming. She said it was a waste of time, and that I had too much work to do to waste time daydreaming. That made me a bit skeptical of thinking too much, dreaming too much, wasting any time at all. Instead, I worked. I worked to get educated. I worked to build a career. I worked to save and buy all of the things I was afraid to dream about. Working did not always work. Situations were always changing. Challenges were always popping up. There never seemed to be enough time or money to get to where I wanted to be.

At the onset of my spiritual journey, I learned to visualize, to see something in my mind and accept it as my reality. I learned not to judge what I wanted but to believe it. I learned not to expend effort and struggle, but to trust and believe. In some cases, the results were remarkable. Things would just show up in my life. Situations would work out. Obstacles would be removed. People would change or disappear, leaving me in peace or shock, depending on the situation. Unfortunately, visualization didn't seem work all the time. I would hit and then miss with my mental picturing before I could hit again. In the interim, while trying to *see my way into* what I wanted, I was *working real hard* to try to make it happen. It was very frustrating.

Where did I want my life to go? What did I want my life to look like? What did I really want in life? I kept changing my mind; perhaps that is why many things did not happen. There were many things that I asked for, only to discover they were not exactly what I had in mind. How are you supposed to ask for something if you are not really sure what it is? How do you grow into your highest potential if you do not know what that potential is? If you ask these questions often enough, you get tired of asking them. You can also get so many answers popping into your mind that eventually you get confused. What I discovered is that there is an answer, one answer that will bring the question of growth and expansion into full expression. Unfortunately, I did not like the answer!

The purpose of this life and all of its experiences is not to make ourselves what we think we should be. It is to unfold as what we already are. We are already powerful, divine, wise, loving beings. We are that way because of the spirit of the Divine within us. That spirit is always seeking expression. We are the vehicles of that expression. As our life's experiences play out, our responsibility is to live up to the inherent qualities of the Divine. In this way, we will grow in our spiritual nature, expand the vision of ourselves, and discover the meaning of life. In order to do this, we must bring ourselves into alignment with divine will and divine purpose. In other words, we must do what it is that the Divine has sent us here to do. I didn't like the thought of that. What if God wanted me to be something I did not want to be. What if God wanted me to do something I did not want to do. There I was, wanting what I wanted again. Holding onto what I thought was right again. Refusing to grow or expand beyond my own limited view of myself into the divine view God held of me and for me. There I was, asking how when the Divine was waiting for me to say yes. I can imagine you have no idea of what I am talking about!

I once heard Marianne Williamson, author of *A Return to Love,* say, "No matter what you can ask for, it is only a microscopic view of what God wants to give you!" That was a smack in my face! Stage and screen actress BarbaraO once said to me, "Rather than asking for the conditional need in the now, ask for the continuous flow into forever." I had never thought about it in that way. Ashamed as I may be to admit it, I have usually begged and pleaded with God to get me out of this or that situation. I had never asked to be kept out of all situations. That is what expansion is about. Expanding your view of who you are and what you deserve to such a degree that you never find yourself in limiting situations again. Now, here's the key. Rather than telling God what you want, ask God to show you what is in store for you, and then ask for guidance in developing in yourself whatever qualities and characteristics will be necessary to make God's vision of you and for you your reality. This is the difference between visualizing and visioning. Telling God what you want and being willing to expand into what God already has for you.

Comedienne Moms Mabley said it best: "If you always do what you've always done, you will always get what you've always got." We owe it to ourselves to expand our vision of who we are. We owe it to the Divine to expand our sense of what we can do. I now realize that there have been many situations in my life in which I have fought to hold onto reasons and excuses for not being where I wanted to be. It is always easy to blame others. It is even easier to find a perfectly logical excuse for not growing, expanding, or being all that you want to be. I have probably used every excuse and trick in the book to give myself a reason not to do better than I was doing. One day I decided to take a risk. You must be willing to risk losing everything if you are serious about getting anything. I risked my life, my resources, my need to be right, and the fear of being afraid, and asked God to show me myself as God saw me. The vision was so spectacular, I have spent the last twelve years of my life running to keep up with all the good things that have been happening. And, you know what? None of what I am experiencing is what I asked for, and all of it is better than I would have ever dared to ask for. It is called expansion into the Divine.

Commentary Journal

After reading today's commentary, I realize

The key phrase(s) I want to remember and work with today are

Morning EXPANSION Affirmation

I am willing to become more of life.

I am willing to receive more of what life has to offer.

I have no fear of seeing myself, knowing myself, being my divine self.

I am willing to EXPAND beyond the limits I have placed on myself and those that I have allowed others to place upon me.

I am willing to EXPAND my understanding of the truth, my experience of joy, and my demonstrations of love.

I now ask the Holy Spirit for the necessary guidance to EXPAND my vision into the realization of all the divine good that life has in store for me.

For this I am so grateful!

And So It Is!

Let Me Remember . . .

God only wants the best for me.

God knows what is best for me.

I am willing to see myself as God sees me.

No matter what I ask, God has more in store.

God cannot give me what I want if I do not know what it is.

Taking a risk on God is divine.

Evening EXPANSION Journal

I congratulate myself for having an EXPANDED vision as it relates to

I now realize the areas of my life which are not EXPANDING are

I am now willing to experience EXPANSION in my life in order to experience

DAY 37

Honor Life
with . . . GRATITUDE

Working Definition:

The principle we are working with today is GRATITUDE. It is the recognition and expression of appreciation for what is. Thanksgiving for what is and what is received. An attitude of acknowledgment.

Commentary on GRATITUDE

Someone once asked me, "When was the last time somebody gave you something valuable and expected nothing in return?" This person went on to say that valuable did not necessarily mean expensive. As a matter of fact, valuable in this case meant priceless. I really had to think about it. Most of the things I considered priceless, I had received from my children. Many of these things were not even tangible. Things they had said to me or done for me, I considered priceless, but there was usually an expectation of them receiving something in return—even if it was a thank you. I responded that I could not remember. As I said it, a fleeting thought passed through my mind: "God did. God gave you life, and you weren't required to do anything to get it, nor did He expect anything in return." Just as the words ceased in my mind, the person talking to me said the exact same thing. "God did."

It makes no sense to complain about the wrapping paper when you know that there is a gift inside. We like pretty wrapping paper, with matching bows and nice cards. When a gift is nicely wrapped, we take our time to open it. We don't want to mishandle the paper. Because it looks pretty on the outside we anticipate there is something just as nice on the inside. This is not always the case with the gifts we receive, and it is certainly not the case with the life we have received. The experiences and conditions of life are the wrappings; they are not the essence, the invaluable gift. Many of the things we complain about, worry about, create drama about, and fear in life are simply ugly wrapping paper. They may not be pleasant to look at or live through, but they do not affect the essence of life. When we think about the true meaning and value of the gift of life, the only worthy response is gratitude. As expressed here, gratitude is more than a word or a gesture. Being truly grateful for the gift of life must be an experience.

At the age of forty I became extremely depressed about all I had done and not done. I was always doing something or forgetting to do something. The minute I stopped doing one thing, I had to find something else to do. At times, I found no satisfaction in what I had done, so I kept doing. It is very easy to get so wrapped up in *doing* what you feel needs to be done that you forget to be grateful for the ability *to do*. To walk. To breathe. To think. These are gifts. To see. To hear. To feel. These are invaluable gifts. Each of these gifts is an inherent element of the life we have done nothing to receive, and we are asked for nothing in return. These gifts are so liberally bestowed upon us that there are times when we act like spoiled children. We take our gifts for granted. We are ungrateful.

We must learn to experience gratitude as an experience of being alive. When we become grateful to this degree we will begin to notice the small things. Things like the blinking of our eyes, our hair growing, our skin stretching when we move our bodies in the act of doing. When you are grateful you listen to the beating of your heart. You marvel at the growth of your finger- and toenails. You acknowledge everything that you have; more important, you recognize who you are. You are a living expression of the Creator of the universe. You are twenty-two trillion cells, and within each of those cells there are millions of molecules. Each molecule of your being contains an atom oscillating at more than ten million times each second. All of this activity is controlled by a three-pound brain that contains thirteen billion cells that control four million pain-sensitive structures, five hundred thousand touch detectors, and two hundred thousand temperature detectors. If someone gave you a brand-new car for your birthday, you would probably be very grateful. If, however, you left that car outside for two years, five years, or ten years, it would rust and fall apart. You, on the other hand, never rust. Are you grateful for the activity of life in your body and brain that keeps you from rusting?

Gratitude is a state of consciousness. It is an experience of living in a state of joy. I have watched the expressions on the faces of people caught in a traffic jam. I see how irritated they become. I watch them trying to weave in and out to get to somewhere. I often wonder how many of them are grateful to be in a car? How many of them are grateful that they have a watch that informs them that they are about to be late? Gratitude means living without the fear of death. We can become so preoccupied with dying—when we will die, what we must do before we die, who will take of this or that after we die—that we forget to live fully right now, in the moment we have. If you choose to live in panic, drama, and fear, life will accommodate you! It will give you exactly what is required to experience your chosen state of mind. If you want to live peacefully, joyfully, and abundantly, you must choose to discover these experiences as often as you can, and you must be grateful for them. My father always said, "You must want what you have before you can have what you want." Gratitude is like a magnet that attracts more of it to itself; the more grateful you are, the more you will receive to be grateful for.

Electricity does not care if you believe in it or not. When you want to experience light in a dark room, the only requirement is that you flip the switch. The electric current moving through the wires does not care if you like it, if you know how it works, if you believe in its power. The light responds to the connection of the circuits that happens when you flip the switch. Life works the same way. It does not care if you like it. Life is not concerned about convincing you that it is good or abundant. Life will not stop because you do not believe in it. And whether you believe in life or not, you will not rust or fall apart if you stand still for five years. The only requirement for you to live a full and valuable life is for you to flip the switch, to make the connection. Gratitude is the connection between who and what you are and the full magnificence of life.

Commentary Journal

After reading today's commentary, I realize

The key phrase(s) I want to remember and work with today are

Morning GRATITUDE Affirmation

I am so GRATEFUL to be alive.

I am GRATEFUL for every gift and ability life affords me.

*I am GRATEFUL for each and every experience I have had that has made
    my life what it is today.*

I am GRATEFUL for the lessons I have learned.

I am GRATEFUL for the opportunity to learn more.

*I am GRATEFUL to be an expression of the divine life moving in me and
    through me.*

I am GRATEFUL to be awake.

I am GRATEFUL to have a consciousness.

*I am GRATEFUL that my life can be a reflection of divine consciousness
    at any given moment.*

*I am GRATEFUL that today is the only opportunity I need to live in the
    fullness of joy, peace, and unlimited abundance.*

*Today, I will plant seeds of GRATITUDE in my life, knowing and
    believing that they will bloom to the goodness and glory of the Divine.*

I am so GRATEFUL! I am so GRATEFUL! I am so GRATEFUL!

For all I have received and all that is yet to come!

And So It Is!

Let Me Remember . . .

To be GRATEFUL because life is an invaluable gift.

To be GRATEFUL because I am a living instrument of the divine.

To be GRATEFUL for the miraculous inner workings of my being.

To be GRATEFUL for every experience that has brought me to this day.

To be GRATEFUL for everything I have ever received.

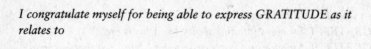

Evening GRATITUDE Journal

I congratulate myself for being able to express GRATITUDE as it relates to

I recognize that it is difficult to be GRATEFUL when

I recognize that I can easily express GRATITUDE when

DAY
38

Honor Life
with . . . ORDER

Working Definition:

The principle we are working with today is ORDER. It is adjustment to universal harmony. Alignment. Perfect and timely manifestation. Proper placement.

Commentary on ORDER

1,2,3,4,5. Monday, Tuesday, Wednesday. Summer, Fall, Winter, Spring. Conception, development, delivery. There is a natural order to everything in life. Life is not stagnant. It unfolds and develops in an orderly manner. At times, the order seems disorderly, illogical, and irrational. Consider the pain associated with birth or the destruction that follows a storm. The purpose of the pain or the storm may not make sense to the logical and rational mind. Yet things always seem to fall into place, to become ordered, no matter how disruptive they appear at first to be.

You and I are evidence of the orderly development of the process of life. We have grown physically, mentally, emotionally, and spiritually according to the orderly unfolding of our life experiences. I admit that there were many times when I and my life appeared to be in total disorder. Now I realize how that disorder was ordered according to my choices and developmental needs. There is a divine order and a physical order that impacts each of us according to the divine plan of divine will. We must each learn and remember what we need to learn and remember about our divine identity. Our steps are ordered by our choices. Our choices are ordered by our experiences. Our experiences are ordered by the divine purpose for our lives. The purpose, for each of us, is to remember to trust the divine process of life.

Order is the grace of God that brings to us exactly what we need, exactly when we need it. God's grace assures us that the divine plan for our lives will unfold in an orderly manner according to our level of development. How many times have you convinced yourself that you were ready for something only to discover later, sometimes painfully, that you were in fact not ready? Perhaps you missed a step or two along the way. Perhaps you were not aware of everything that would be required of you. You stepped out. You fell down. That too was in order. You needed to know what you did not know so that you could prepare yourself for the next experience.

There is another kind of order with which we must also be familiar. It is physical order. The order of the physical environment is a reflection of the order or state of the mind. A clear and open mind is usually evidenced by a clean and orderly environment. The condition or order of the environment demonstrates what you have learned, what you are thinking, and what you are ready to receive. Is your environment cluttered? Is it run-down or unkept? Is it full of stuff? Is the stuff in ill repair? Take a look around the room you are in, your home, your office, your car, and ask yourself, "Is this place a true reflection of what I think about me? Is this place a reflection of what I actually believe and feel about myself?" If it is, good for you! If it is not, then ask, "What must I be thinking to allow myself to be in a place like this?" The place in which you find yourself physically, mentally, or emotionally is a reflection of the order or disorder in your thoughts, beliefs, and emotions. The question we must constantly ask ourselves is, "Am I in order or out of order according to my level of development?"

Order is more than having a place for everything and having everything in its place. While that is a good place to start, order is also the ability to recognize that *you are* in order, and that where you find yourself is where you need to be. We become bored by doing repetitive tasks. Once we have mastered something, we want to move on. There are times when we believe that the things we are asked to do are beneath us, and other times we believe we are ill equipped to do what we are asked to. God's grace is order, and you are in the presence of grace at all times. There is a divine reason you are where you are. Perhaps there is something you have forgotten to do or practice. Is there an ability, skill, or virtue you have not been practicing lately? Maybe you are not ready to move on and this situation has come to let you know just that. If you really believe you are not where you need to be, what are you willing to do to get there? Could it be that the order of the events in which you now find yourself is the orderly unfolding of your divine development? What do you know that you need to be doing that you are not doing? Could this be an opportunity for you to do it? Every experience is ordered by grace to teach and remind us of who we are in the divine scheme of things.

You can put your mind in order by focusing on one thing at a time, doing it well, and appreciating the opportunity for preparation that this doing offers. You can put your life in order by admitting to yourself what you really want to experience, and taking one step at a time that will move you closer to that experience. You can put your environment in order by clearing out the old, worn-out, broken, and useless things that are taking up space. You can put your spirit in order by replacing fearful, doubtful, angry thoughts with thoughts about the grace of God, and by accepting that God's purpose, plan, and will for you is the orderly development of your soul's identity.

Commentary Journal

After reading today's commentary, I realize

The key phrase(s) I want to remember and work with today are

Morning ORDER Affirmation

Today, I ask the Holy Spirit to order my thoughts, my words, my steps, and my life.

Today, I desire to recognize and realize God's grace in every experience.

Today, I am willing to be shaped and molded according to God's perfect plan for my life.

Today, I will seek the truth about myself, accept the truth about myself, and live the truth of my being.

Today, I acknowledge that God's grace is at the head of my life and that all is well.

For this I am so grateful!

And So It Is!

Let Me Remember . . .

ORDER is God's grace.

Where I am is where I need to be in ORDER to learn or remember.

ORDER begins in the spirit and flows to the mind.

ORDER flows from preparation.

My thoughts are ORDERED by God.

My steps are ORDERED by God

My life is ORDERED by my choices.

Evening ORDER Journal

I congratulate myself for taking steps toward bringing ORDER to

Today, I recognized disorder in my life when

Today, I realized that my life is being ORDERED when

DAY 39

Honor Life with . . . Joy

Working Definition:

The principle we are working with today is JOY. It is a state of delight and well-being. An experience of great pleasure. Inner jubilation demonstrated as a pleasant manner. A state of happiness.

Commentary on Joy

Joy and happiness are not the same thing. Joy is an internal process grounded in knowledge of spiritual truth, the ability to trust the wisdom of the Divine, and faith in the perfect and perfecting process of life. Happiness is generally a mental and emotional response to temporary external stimulation, in response to a perceived need. Joy is a state of being. Happiness is a demonstration or expression reliant on a series of events that may or may not occur. Joy is emotional stimulation in response to spiritual inspiration. Happiness is mental inspiration in response to physical stimulation. Do they look alike? Yes. Do they feel alike? Sometimes. Do joy and happiness reap the same results in your life? Absolutely not! Joy, because it is grounded in the spirit, has a more far-reaching and lasting impact. Happiness, which is more often than not based on something physical and tangible, can come and go, moment to moment.

Joy is *knowing* that everything is okay right now. Happiness is *hoping* that it will be soon. Joy is the ability to recognize and discern the truth. Happiness is trying to figure out what is true from what is false. When you figure it out, you are happy. When you do not or cannot figure it out, happiness escapes you.

Joy stays with you no matter where you are and what is going on. Happiness is a response to where you are and what happens to you while you are there. Joy is the knowledge of unconditional love. Happiness is the quest for temporary pleasure. Can you have joy without happiness? No. Can you have happiness without joy? For a brief time, yes. Can joy lead to happiness? Almost always does. Can happiness lead to joy? Absolutely not! Whenever your state of being is dependent on external factors, it is temporary and not joyous.

Joy is the ability to stand in the knowledge of spiritual truth in the face of any and all physical experiences. Does that mean you will be smiling all the time? No. Does it mean you will feel good all the time? No. Does it mean you will never again experience a moment of fear, doubt, shame, guilt, anger, or loneliness? Absolutely not! It means that when you are challenged by these pesky little varmints, what you *know* will shake you, slap you, rise to the surface, and remind you that there *is a strength in you* that nothing and no one can take. Your strength will become your guidance, your protection, and your salvation. Joy is the willingness to keep moving no matter what. Joy is courage to boldly go where you are advised not to go. Joy is the freedom and ability to make conscious choices in the face of seeming disaster, by accepting and acknowledging that you are a creative being on a divine journey, and that nothing but the Divine can stop you. Happiness does not give you the power to choose, create, or sustain yourself when your back is up against the wall and the wolves are snapping at you! Joy, by virtue of its spiritual nature, gives you the ability to stare the wolves down.

It is difficult to be happy when everyone around you is sad. This is why we need joy. It can be quite challenging to remain happy when you face the unknown, unexpected, unplanned events of life. This is why we must develop a sense of inner joy. When the job disappears, the marriage goes sour, the children act up, the car breaks down, all in one day—a day when there is fifteen inches of snow on the ground, and your best friend is out of town—you will have to reach real far to find something to be happy about. If, on the other hand, all of this is going on and you have joy in your heart, you will remember the words of the old spiritual, "It will be all over in the morning!" Even if the morning is days, weeks, months, or years in coming, joy can sustain you for as long as it takes. When you get right down to it, happiness is a sense of feeling full in response to the circumstances and events of life. Joy is a state of being fulfilled simply because you are alive. The difference between joy and happiness may seem like a very small thing, but when the wolves start chasing you, it can make a very big difference in whether you get away or if you are eaten up.

Commentary Journal

After reading today's commentary, I realize

The key phrase(s) I want to remember and work with today are

Morning JOY Affirmation

I am JOYOUSLY JOY-filled.
I am JOY in motion.
I am JOY in action.
I am on a JOYFUL mission to spread more JOY!
I walk in the light of JOY!
I move in the presence of JOY!
I create moments of JOY for myself and those around me!
The more I am, the more I become!
JOY is what I am!
JOY is what I give!
JOY is what I create, attract and use to sustain myself at every moment of
the day!
The JOY of the Divine is my strength! My guide! My desire! My
protection!
For this I am so grateful!
And So It Is!

Let Me Remember . . .

JOY is a state of being.

JOY is spiritually inspired.

JOY begins within.

JOY is not dependent on people or circumstances.

JOY has a lasting effect.

The JOY of the Divine is for me to have JOY.

Evening JOY Journal

I congratulate myself for remaining in a state of JOY when

I now realize I have not been JOYFUL because

I will remember to remain JOYFUL when

Honor Life with . . .
UNCONDITIONAL LOVE

Working Definition:

The principle we are working with today is UNCONDITIONAL LOVE. It is acknowledgment and acceptance of the presence of God. Selfless giving. Openness to receiving.

Commentary on Unconditional Love

If someone had told me that I knew nothing about unconditional love, I would have dismissed them as a lunatic. After all, I was the author of four books on spiritual matters. I had experienced a total transformation in my consciousness and my life that I openly attributed to the activity of God's unconditional love in my life. I had conducted workshops, seminars, and given lectures across the country on a wide variety of matters and topics, all of which were based on the concept of unconditional love. I thought that I was unconditional love in heels! Then into my life walked a man who declared unconditional love for me. I immediately went into shock, fear, and a mode of self-destruct.

The Course teaches, "There is only one love, and it is God's unconditional love." Perhaps it is also in *The Course in Miracles* where I have read, "Love will bring up anything unlike itself." What I have discovered is that when you come face to face with unconditional love, it not only brings up in your being every unloving feeling and thought; unconditional love will shake those things in your face and dare you to deny that they do not belong to you! It is hard to tell a lie when God's love is staring at you. It is even harder to admit that you have been lying to yourself all along.

When the male person to whom I alluded earlier declared his commitment to and unconditional love for me, I began to find as many things wrong with him as possible. Something had to be wrong with him! Why else would he want me? I never said any of this to him, instead I conjured up in my own mind a million and one ways he would demonstrate his wrongness. I was on the lookout for any little thing that would prove that I was right about him. He refused to play into my trap. He kept his word. He showed up on time. He whispered sweet nothings in my ear. He took every opportunity available to demonstrate his care and concern for me. When there was no apparent opportunity, he made one. He told the absolute truth, under all circumstances, and he told me all the things about himself that he thought I needed to know. It was a trick! A low-down dirty trick! He was wrong! I was right! Unfortunately, there was no evidence to prove it.

When my powers of observation began to fail me, I took a new approach. I began to criticize him. I treated his kind and loving deeds with total indifference. When that didn't work, I began to question his motives, his character, his family background! He was good to his mother. Although divorced, he was a conscious and participatory father. He was on a spiritual journey to strengthen and develop himself for no other reason but to be strengthened and developed. He liked politics, sports, and music. He loved children, flowers, and quiet time to read. He helped old ladies across the street. He opened the car door for me and held the door open for those who were coming in behind him. He had a hearty laugh, and he was not afraid to cry, in the open, when he was happy or sad. This man, this wonderful and divine expression of love, wanted me to be his wife. I concluded that he had to be a stark, raving maniac!

When you have lived most of your life believing there is something terribly wrong with you, unconditional love will show you the truth. When you are able to convince yourself that no matter what you do, you still are not good enough, unconditional love will show you the truth. When you give the demands of your ego and your very human habits catchy little new-age names, unconditional love will strip away everything you are hiding, dangle it before your eyes, and quietly whisper to you, "How are you going to deal with this, sweetie?" He accepted my criticisms because he trusted me. He went along with my mood swings because he realized "creative people are a little different." He gave me the space I asked for when I asked for it. He shared everything he had without apologizing that he didn't have more to give. He acknowledged his own shortcomings and accepted mine as a part of who I was. Each time I pointed out to him my frailties, weaknesses, and physical imperfections, quietly and gently he reminded, "That's what I love about you most!"

I had done everything I could possibly think of to drive him away, but he would not go. Finally, when the demons of my ego were about to make me do something very foolish, something like call off the wedding, I took myself to task. *What the hell is wrong with you? Is this not what you have been praying, asking, begging for? Go get your journal, your love list, your treasure map! Look how many times you have asked for a loving, support-ive mate. A gentle, spiritual, fun-loving man with whom to share your life. How many relationships have you ended because the guy did not live up to your expectations? Now here you have a man who fits the bill exactly and you are trying to find something wrong with him! You are beating him up for being and doing everything you said you wanted a man to be and do! Well, he could have a little more money! Shut up! You could have a little more love! For yourself and for him, but most of all for God!*

This is God in your face, asking nothing of you and giving you every-thing He has. This is the activity of God's unconditional love moving you out of fear, out of your self-imposed limitations, out of the temporary lust of your physical mind into the unexplored territory of your heart. Are you open to that experience, or have you been giving lip service to it? Are you afraid that you cannot control what is going on so you want to run away from it? Are you afraid that all of the garbage you have been telling your-self about your self is just that, garbage? Are you afraid to discover that all the things you have told yourself about God and about love are actually true? When there is a battle going on in your mind, some part of you will be forced to surrender, forced to tell the truth, forced to give up the strong-hold it has had on your mind. In the pursuit or presence of unconditional love you must surrender, you must tell the truth, you must let go of the ego. My readiness was evidenced by my response. Quietly I allowed myself to answer, yes, I was afraid to be loved unconditionally.

Where love is, there is no fear. For just a moment I allowed myself to feel the presence of God's unconditional love. In that presence, I remembered all the things I thought were wrong about me, and miraculously they all seemed to fade away. In the presence, I confessed to myself all the things I had done of which I was not proud, the things about which I was either ashamed or guilty. Suddenly everything had a meaning. I could see how I had grown through those behaviors and experiences. In the presence of God's unconditional love, I found the courage to admit to myself what I really wanted in my life, and that I was afraid to have it. My fears were based in my parental programming, my behavior patterns, my people-pleasing tendencies, my self-defeating attitudes. As I felt myself slipping back into the grips of my ego, I heard a quiet voice from within my being say, *"Come unto Me. There is no love but my love. In the presence of my love all that is not love will fade."*

A condition is something that we believe will make something better than it already is. There is nothing that we can ever want or need that will make God's love any better than it already is. There is nothing we can ever do that will make God stop loving us. God's love is unconditional. It is present everywhere, at all times. The only challenge we face in recognizing and receiving God's love is the demand of the ego.

The ego is the dark, shadowy side of us that wants us to believe we are not capable of being loved by anyone, particularly not by God. The ego keeps us in shame, guilt, and confusion about our true identity. The ego keeps us resistant to telling the truth, and then uses our internal and external display of dishonesty to breed fear in our hearts. Unconditional love of self and others is the only way to dismantle the ego. It requires that we accept and acknowledge the truth about ourselves and about God. It demands that we honor God by honoring ourselves. Unconditional love is understanding that no matter what we do or how we behave, God loves us, and is waiting for us to embody and demonstrate love at all times, under all circumstances. After forty-three years of ego-based living, God answered my prayers, showing up in my life as a husband who loves me unconditionally. There are times when I still forget who I am and who he is. There are still times when I fall into the traps of my ego. Each day I become aware of the attitudes and behaviors I display that are fear-based, judgmental, controlling, and unloving. When I recognize these things about myself, I admit them to myself, and call forth the presence and energy of divine, unconditional love. In that presence, I am reminded to simply be willing to change and the change will unfold naturally.

After reading today's commentary, I realize

The key phrase(s) I want to remember and work with today are

Morning UNCONDITIONAL LOVE Affirmation

The energy in which I live, move, and have my being is God's UNCONDITIONAL LOVE.

The power that permeates every atom, cell, and molecule of my being is God's UNCONDITIONAL LOVE.

The reality through which my life is unfolding is God's UNCONDITIONAL LOVE.

There is no energy greater than God's UNCONDITIONAL LOVE.

There is no power stronger than God's UNCONDITIONAL LOVE.

There is no reality that I desire to know more than God's UNCONDITIONAL LOVE.

As I accept, acknowledge, and embrace God's UNCONDITIONAL LOVE, it becomes the guiding force of my life.

For this I am so grateful!

And So It Is!

Let Me Remember . . .

There is only one love, God's love.

God's love for me is UNCONDITIONAL.

Where there is UNCONDITIONAL LOVE there is no fear.

God loves me no matter what.

*I congratulate myself for being able to express UNCONDITIONAL
LOVE today when*

I acknowledge that I have been placing conditions on love by

*I am willing to experience UNCONDITIONAL LOVE in all areas of my
life because*

Phase Seven

There came a day and time in my life when I could relate everything I heard, saw, or experienced to the goodness and glory of the divine presence of God. The title of my favorite song, "In a Sentimental Mood," became "In a Spiritual Mood." The words "I never imagined you would be loving a sentimental me" were transformed to "I can only imagine You loving the spirit in me." The pulsating and seductive words of songs like "You Make Me Feel Like a Natural Woman" and "I Never Knew Love Like This" took on meanings completely different than the ones the songwriters envisioned. Gone were the images of a tall, handsome, wealthy man. They were replaced by the desire to consciously realize and know the presence of God. The words of Guru Muktananda, "When you eat you are feeding God. When you speak, you are speaking for God and to God. When you live, you are living the glory of God," became a truth and a reality of my life. Yes. There were moments, even days, when I still found myself rushing around in fear, falling prey to the beliefs of inadequacy and worthiness fostered by the ego. However, the truth would eventually burst through in my mind, reminding me of my spiritual inheritance and identity. I am a natural woman! Constantly being loved and embraced by the spirit of God! What a blessing!

There came a time and a moment in my life when the fear of death, failure, and ridicule were replaced by acknowledgment of my ability to choose and create, choose and re-create. I wrote on an index card, *"I have no fear of seeing my Self, knowing my Self, being my Self."* I placed that card on the windowsill in my bathroom. It was the first thing I saw every morning. I saw myself in people, in events, in the circumstances of my life that often showed up cleverly disguised as people who didn't like me or care about me. I showed up as lack of resources. Often I appeared as something I did not want to see or know or face. When I showed up like that in my life, I would choose again by re-creating my thoughts and feelings about the part of me that I was facing. Suddenly, miraculously, the person, circumstance, or situation would look different. I realized it was because I felt differently about me and how I was showing up.

There came a time in my life, a moment, when I became willing to open my heart to feel, know, and experience love. Not the love of my husband or my children. Rather, I became willing to accept the fact that God loved me. God loved the frightened little girl in me who had told lies and stolen money. God loved the rebellious teenager in me who had been defiant, promiscuous, angry, and confused. I became willing to acknowledge that God loved me no matter what I had done or why I had done it. I realized that God's love was the breath I was breathing. It was the blood running through my veins. God's love was the beating of my heart, and the systematic functioning of vital organs and systems in body. These were all indications of God's love. God knew that I farted and belched, and still God loved me. It was on that day, in that moment, that it all became clear. The principles of life were my parents. The laws of God, which gave birth to the principles of life, were my guidance counselors. The love of God, from which the laws sprang to give birth to life's principles, were the foundation of my existence. It finally became clear that God was not out to get me or punish me. I realized that the divine activity and presence of God were always guiding me, encouraging me to make better choices and decisions, to remain open to love, not to judge myself, but to embrace all of me, and most of all, not to shift into fear when I forgot to do any of these. It finally became clear that my eyes, ears, hands, feet, and body were all divine instruments of God, and that my only job in this life was to acknowledge myself as a divine instrument and to be grateful for the opportunity to use my divine energy to create a better life for myself and others.

A truly wonderful thing happens when you get clear. Gone is the need to be right, to be the best, to move fast, and to outdo others. Clarity gives you the ability to do what you are doing, to the best of your ability, without being afraid that you are doing the wrong thing. You are no longer doing, you are being. Clarity fosters the blessed and divine ability to like everything about yourself, knowing that it is all good, and that it is all God. God wants us to know who we are by discovering who we are not. The experiences of who we are do not make us very clear about who we are. With that degree of clarity, we find the courage and strength to move out of the confines and limitations of fear into the alignment of our soul with the principles of God's purpose. When you are clear, the opinion you trust is your own. The creative ability you aspire to demonstrate is your own. The gratitude you express is to your self for your ability to recognize and embrace your truth as the method for reminding you of who and what you are not. Clarity gives you patience with yourself. It fosters discipline in your mind. It teaches you to love everything and everyone as a reflection of you and the areas you must still work to develop and strengthen in your self. Clarity is worth more than all the gold in all the storehouses of all the lands in all civilizations. Clarity removes all the boundaries from your mind and heart, moving you into the realization that you are in fact divine. With that knowledge, your sanity is restored, your divinity is activated, and life becomes an outgrowth of the knowledge of the truth of your being. Speaking for myself, when things became that crystal clear to me, my soul opened up, and the peace, joy, and love of God poured in. I have never been the same nor do I choose to be.

Like many of my human brothers and sisters, I spent far too much of my life struggling with the demons in myself. Unworthiness. Inadequacy. Fear. Valuelessness. Arrogance. Lack of discipline. Disobedience. Wanting to be special while refusing to admit that was what I actually wanted. I was spiritually schizophrenic. I wanted the best that life had to offer, but I was afraid to admit it. I thought I was being selfish and greedy, and that the things I wanted were unattainable because I was bad and unworthy. I was at war with and in my own world, the one I had unconsciously created. Pushing myself to do more while mentally and emotionally sabotaging my efforts. I could talk myself into believing that almost anything good was possible, and just as quickly talk myself out of it. This battle went on for more than twenty years. It was a bloody battle that left pieces of me lying bloody by the side of life's road. It was a vicious battle in which I created and used many violent weapons to beat myself over the head. When the battle was just about over, the demons just about to claim their victory over me, I found the presence of mind to offer up to that vengeful, punishing, picky God I believed in, the ultimate prayer, "HELP!" True to God's form, of which I had been totally oblivious, S/He answered my prayer. The words of my father rang aloud in my ears: "SIT DOWN! SHUT UP! LISTEN!"

I know you and I love you! I know everything there is to know about you because I created everything that you are! I wish you would give me a little credit! I who made everything from nothing can certainly make something of all that I AM in you! I can heal your self-inflicted wounds. I can correct your mindless mistakes. I can alter the course you have chosen in fear by revealing the path I have given you with and in love. I can pick you up when you fall. I can come to where you have fallen and give you what you need to get up on your own. I can listen and I can talk, do talk all the time. I am not limited by time or distance. I AM not hindered by opinion polls or public sentiment. I have a plan because I AM the plan. There is nothing you have that I need, and everything you need I have because I created it all. Now, you have asked for help. I can help you. I have helped you. I do help you, and I will help you now that you have asked. There is nothing I ask in return. I ask not that you give back to me what I have given to you because I already own it all. I simply remind you of one thing. If you truly want my help, you must get out of my way! Lay down the fear, the anger, the hatred, the limitations that you place on my help. Open your mind and heart to give love and be love in everything that you think, do, and say. Stop putting me on a schedule of when to help, and telling me whom to help and why I should help. If you truly want my help, listen to me when I speak through others. Listen to me in music, in the wind, and most of all in the silence. If you actually want my help, come to me in your heart and ask for it, just as you have just done. Each time you do, because you will do it again, know that I AM here and that I will answer. When I do, have the courage to listen!

As I wiped the tears from my eyes and dragged my body up from the floor, one thought permeated my mind: "Well! That was about as clear as it can get!" The new battle was to figure out how to stay clear.

A Clear Day

I could have written this entire book in five pages. Unfortunately, the publisher would not have considered it a book, and you probably would have thought it was too simple to have any real validity. We like it hard. We like to drag things out. We like to agree and disagree. Argue and debate. Pick apart every little thing to see if it matches what we believe, have heard, and have been told. We forget how to appreciate simplicity because it is simply too simple to be true. I am grateful for the opportunity to present in three hundred pages what I could have stated in five. It has helped me to remember some things I tend to forget. It has helped me to practice some things I had laid aside. I was promised help whenever I needed it.

I am also grateful for the opportunity to share with others the challenges I have discovered in being human. It helps me to remember my oneness with you. In that oneness I am strengthened and encouraged. I know that I am not alone in the quest to get and stay clear about my true identity. I know I am not alone on the journey to spiritual strength and personal joy. You, holding this book in your hand, help me remember that truth. However, I also know how challenging it can be to try to remember everything we read and apply to the situations we face every day. For that reason alone I feel the need to condense into a few pages what I have written in all those that have preceded.

Tell the Truth

My grandmother said this to me every day for the first ten years of my life. She seemed to have some kind of radar that let her know when I was being dishonest. I remember how she would chastise me for doing something and turn her back. I would immediately make a face or stick my tongue out at her. Without skipping a step or turning around, she would ask, "Are you sassing me?" Without so much as a thought, I would respond, "No!" That was not the truth, but I thought if I told her, "Yes, Grandma, I just stuck my tongue out at you," I would get in trouble. How many times do we fail to tell the truth in fear of the trouble it will bring? Tell the truth about what you are feeling. Tell the truth about what you are thinking. Tell the truth about what you are doing and why you are doing it. It is only when you tell the truth to yourself about yourself that you can get the help you need to bring yourself into alignment with God's true purpose for you.

Be Obedient

"Do what you are told to do!" is how Grandma put it. It comes to you as a thought. It grows into a desire. It permeates your every waking hour, leading you through your days and nights. That thing you want that won't let you go. Those things your mind tells you you must do in order to be free. Be obedient to your mind when it speaks to you. Listen to your thoughts because they are the higher calling. BE OBEDIENT! If you are like me, you probably wonder how to know when this thing you are thinking about is what you are supposed to do. Here are a few guidelines: Will the thing bring you joy without harm to yourself or anyone else? Will the thing bring some good to yourself or the rest of the world? Will the thing move you beyond some fear you now hold about doing it? If you answer yes, BE OBEDIENT! Rather than asking, "How can I?" Simply say, "I am willing!"

Discipline Your Mind, Your Body, Your Being!

Why did you get up this morning? What do you hope to experience by the end of this day? In order to answer these questions and put yourself in alignment with divine purpose in your life, you must have discipline. You must do what you say you will do when you say you will do it. You must consciously and creatively structure your day toward some small intention. You must be disciplined in thought, word, and deed. Consciously train yourself to do those things that are good for you. Breathing. Walking.

Eating. Resting. Working. Playing. Listening. Creating. Praying. Meditating. Discipline yourself to speak softly. Discipline yourself to live peacefully. Discipline is the only way to avoid struggle, chaos, and confusion. When you know what you must do, when you must do it, and why you are doing it, things that are not in alignment with your intent seem to fall away. When you are where you intend to be, doing what you intend to do, for a goal or purpose you intend to realize, you are less likely to be knocked off your center square. Discipline calms the mind, opens the heart, and clears the path away from ego toward spirit. When you are disciplined in your quest toward peace, joy, harmony, balance, and expansion, you are spared the confines of fear, anger, resentment, restriction, guilt, and shame. Having discipline is like doing one hundred spiritual sit-ups. It builds your spiritual strength and muscles.

Put Your Life in Order

Order! Order! Order! It is the first law of heaven. It is the method by which you bring the human will into alignment with God's will. In the quest for spiritual strength you must order your mind, your body, and all of your affairs. You must clean out and reorder everything in your environment. Take a peek under your bed, in the closet, in the trunk of your car, in the basement of your home, in the attic, in the garage, in the dresser drawers, in your purse, your wallet, the glove compartment of your car, and the junk drawer in the kitchen. Is there order? Is there a place for everything? Is everything in a place? Are you holding on to things that serve no purpose? Are there broken things you have not taken the time to fix? Are there broken things you have not taken the time to get rid of? Are you saving things from the past hoping to relive them? If the things in your environment are a reflection of what goes on in your mind, ask yourself, "Is my mind well ordered?"

When we do not have order or space in our lives, there is little chance for the will of God to unfold. When we hold onto the past, bringing that baggage into the present, chances are we will be crowded out of the future. When we do not know where anything is, it becomes challenging to find or receive what we are looking for. ORDER! ORDER! ORDER! Cleaning out the closet is a good way to eliminate mental clutter. Cleaning out the basement frees the subconscious mind. Relieving a purse or a wallet of old receipts and useless telephone numbers clears the mind of fear, shame, or guilt, of the opportunities we failed to take advantage of in the past. Ordering your day, to do certain things at certain times, in certain ways, raises your chances of being exactly where you need to be, doing exactly what you need to be doing in order to receive the blessings that the Divine has ordered up for you at that time.

Make Another Choice

When you see that what you are doing, what you have chosen is not working, make another choice. When you discover that what you are thinking or feeling is not bringing forth the thoughts and feelings you desire, make another choice. Regardless of how much time you have spent, or how much energy you have expended doing whatever it is that you are doing, if it is not working for you make another choice! Choosing does not mean you abandon or give up. Choice is not synonymous with being fickle or spaced. Choice simply means that you recognize the conflict, chaos, or pain the first choice has created; you choose to eliminate that experience by making another choice.

Wash Your Hands When You Are Done!

We see signs everywhere, every day, reminding us to wash our hands before we move on to the next experience, and we fail to recognize the spiritual import of the words. Elimination is a spiritual as well as a human experience. When you have eliminated, let go of, released something or someone from your life, wash your hands and move on! When something is over, it is over. There is no need to keep checking to see if it or they are really gone. Flush! Wash your hands and move on. Avoid the human tendency to pick things up and inspect them, twisting and turning to discern what it is, why it is, how it is that you have come to this place at this time. Help is on the way! You will know what you need to know when you need to know it. For right now, tell the truth. It's over! You are finished! It is time to let go! Eliminate! Now, wash your hands and move on to the next thing.

Know That You Know

Self-doubt can easily become the cause of every missed step in life. Self-doubt is the fungus that grows into the cancer of worthlessness and inadequacy. Self-doubt steals dreams, denies hope, and assassinates faith. Know that you know what you are doing. When you do what feels right for you, know that you know it is right for you. When you want more than you have now and are willing to do what it takes to get it, know that what you want is right for you. Know that you are always, at all times, under all situations connected to the awesome, powerful, creative source of life. Know that what God knows, you know. When you cannot figure out why you know what you know or what to do about what you know, know that you can ask for clarity, and know that clarity will come. Knowing that you know is what some people call faith.

Fear Not

There is no greater disservice we commit in this life than living within the grips and confines of fear. My friend and mentor Helen Hannon reminded me of this when she said, "You can't lose!" No matter what happens, you cannot lose. If you let go of something or someone that has been divinely ordained for you, it will come back when you are ready to receive it. If you let go of something or someone that has not been divinely ordained for you, you are making room for the Divine to take its place in your life. There is never a good reason to fear that you are wrong or that you are losing. God in you will not deny Itself. It will be fulfilled. It will be acknowledged. Fear only delays fulfillment. It cannot or does not destroy it. Fear is the insidious activity of the belief that there is something that God cannot do or does not know. It is a covert admission that God cannot be trusted and that God's love is not enough to sustain you. Fear is how we act out our loyalty to family patterns that can eventually become the noose around our necks, that "hang us up" in life. Fear not! Realize that no matter what it is, no matter how you show up, no matter what you are experiencing, you cannot lose because help is on the way.

Do All Things in Love!

In case no one has told you that they love you today, allow me to be the first. I LOVE YOU TODAY! I have always loved you; unfortunately, I did not know it was love. I thought I was just a writer doing what would make my publisher and me wealthy. I did not realize that I was loving myself enough to shed and share the misconceptions I had about myself. I did not understand that it was my love for you and my trust of you that enabled me to reveal the pitfalls of my humanness with you. We each do this every day. We rise from bed and take our too fat, too thin, too old, too young, not good enough, not smart enough, inadequate, worthless selves into the world of work, play, commerce, history, economics, politics because we love each other. We keep showing up behind those counters, in those lines, on those telephones, in those cars, trucks, trains, and buses because we love each other. We are not consciously aware that we are demonstrating love because we are so preoccupied with what is wrong, what we lack, what we could have, should have, would have done if we had more time, more money, greater opportunity. We forget that if we don't show up, somebody, even one somebody would miss what we have to offer, ask, or do that day. We do not recognize that we are love in motion, seeking to reveal itself in many ways under all circumstances. We can remedy this. We can make love and loving a priority in our lives by doing one simple thing. We can replace love with every other word that expresses a need, want, thought, or feeling.

Instead of "I hate you" we can say, "I love you." Instead of "I wish I had more money or time," we can say, "I wish I had more love." Instead of "Look what you did to my car, my life, or my credit report!" say, "Look what you did to my love." By inserting the word love into every statement of discord or disharmony, every intention, every goal, we call forth the spirit of love, which is the active presence of God. In the presence of God, the truth is revealed, order, harmony, and balance are restored, peace is unleashed, and life becomes a purposeful event. Whether you are typing, filing, cooking, cleaning, driving, delivering, teaching, nursing, singing, dancing, knitting, policing, voting, or boating, do it with the intention of demonstrating more love. In the presence of love, everything unloving is revealed, providing us with the opportunity to choose again. When we choose to do everything in love and with love present in our consciousness, we are issuing an invitation to the Holy Spirit to open our souls and reveal more love in our lives.

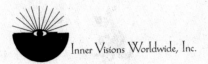 Inner Visions Worldwide, Inc.

Where we believe . . .
"There is a universal power seeking an outlet through you!"

• WORKSHOPS • LECTURES ON TAPE • PRISON MINISTRY •
• CORRESPONDENCE COURSES • SUPPORT GROUPS •
• 24-HOUR PRAYER LINE • CLASSES and other activities •

We invite you to become a member of the
Spiritual Life Maintenance Network

Receive membership discounts on Inner Visions activities and products
Annual Dues $37.50

❑YES! I WOULD LIKE TO BE A MEMBER!

(PLEASE PRINT ALL INFORMATION REQUESTED)

Name: _____

Address: _____

City: _____ State: _____ Zip: _____

Phone: _____ FAX: _____

Form of Payment: ❑ Check/M.O. ❑ Discover ❑ Visa/MC ❑ American Express

Account Number:_____ Expiration Date: _____

Cardholder's Name: _____

Cardholder's Signature_____

✦

❑ I have a friend/family member I would like to enroll in the
INNER VISIONS PRISON MINISTRY.

(Members receive a monthly newsletter and supplementary reading materials.)

Name: _____

Correctional facility: _____

Identification #: _____

Address: _____

City: _____ State: _____ Zip: _____

Enrolled by: _____ Relationship: _____

Please ask prison ministry enrollee to place Inner Visions on the approved mailing list.

Visit our web site at: http://Innervisionsworldwide.com

926 Philadelphia Avenue, Silver Spring, MD 20910 ✦ (301) 608-8750

POCKET
BOOKS

IYANLA VANZANT

'Iyanla Vanzant has used her negative life experiences
to educate herself and liberate others. She is magnanimous and has
chosen to share with others what she has learnt. She offers salvation
to all women who are on the road to self-discovery'
Diane Abbott, MP

'A beautifully packaged, thoughtful little book aimed at
giving reassurance and inspiration'
Now magazine

'A fascinating read . . . I pick it up whenever I'm feeling down
as it's full of inspirational snippets and phrases . . . It's great
to dip into when you want a fresh perspective on things'
Naomi Russell, *Coronation Street*

'Another illuminating instalment for those on
the road to self discovery'
Pride magazine

UNTIL TODAY!
Daily Devotions for Spiritual Growth and Peace of Mind

In the inspiring tradition of *Acts of Faith* – a publishing phenomenon with almost 1 million copies in print – *Until Today!* provides a year's worth of daily inspirational quotes, explanations from Iyanla, and brief exercises or actions for readers to perform. *Until Today!* gives a meaningful but bite-sized foray into a deeper, more satisfying spiritual and emotional life.

PRICE £7.99
ISBN 0 671 03766 8

YESTERDAY, I CRIED
Celebrating the Lessons of Living and Loving

What is the lesson in abuse, neglect, abandonment, rejection? Bestselling author Iyanla Vanzant has had an amazing and difficult life which has unmasked her wonderful gifts and led to wisdom gained. Now she uses her own personal experiences to show how life's hardships can be re-languaged to become lessons that teach us as we grow, heal and learn to love.

PRICE £7.99
ISBN 0 671 02968 1

IN THE MEANTIME
Finding Yourself and the Love You Want

Most of us go through life with a vision of what the ideal relationship is supposed to be, yet too often our longing for a soul mate leads to disappointment and heartbreak. What we see, desire, or harshly judge in our mate is but a reflection of self, Vanzant explains, as she helps us to break free of our fantasies and view a relationship as an ongoing process of discovery and growth.

PRICE £7.99
ISBN 0 671 03399 9

LIVING THROUGH THE MEANTIME
Learning to Break the Patterns of the Past and Begin the Healing

Living Through the Meantime takes you through a process of mental, emotional, and spiritual housecleaning and leads you to deeper levels of consciousness. It's a simple, inspiring guide, perfect for anyone who needs to get his or her own spiritual house in order before inviting someone to share it with them.

PRICE £9.99
ISBN 0 7432 2710 7

EVERY DAY I PRAY
Awakening to the Grace of Inner Communion

Every Day I Pray is a collection of prayers culled from Iyanla's personal journals with ten beautiful black and white photographs of Iyanla at home with her family. As in all of Iyanla's books, she talks about a higher spiritual power with many different names and in offering the meditations and celebrations she has written and collected over the years, Iyanla shares the moving words she uses to communicate with her Higher Power and find her own inner strength.

PRICE £7.99
ISBN 0 7434 5074 4

DON'T GIVE IT AWAY!
A Workbook of Self Affirmation for Young Women

In *Don't Give It Away!*, Vanzant responds to the dozens of letters and e-mails she has received from young women who ask for help in their daily struggle for spiritual guidance and awareness. Iyanla motivates teenage girls to stay focused, love themselves first, and reflect that love back to others.

PRICE £6.99
ISBN 0 684 86983 7